RESEARCHING YOUR WAY TO A GOOD JOB

RESEARCHING YOUR WAY TO A GOOD JOB

Karmen N. T. Crowther

John Wiley & Sons, Inc.
New York ▪ Chichester ▪ Brisbane ▪ Toronto ▪ Singapore

In recognition of the importance of preserving what has been written, it is a policy of John Wiley & Sons, Inc., to have books of enduring value published in the United States printed on acid-free paper, and we exert our best efforts to that end.

This publication is designed to provide accurate and authoritative information in regard to the subject matter covered. It is sold with the understanding that the publisher is not engaged in rendering legal, accounting, or other professional services. If legal advice or other expert assistance is required, the services of a competent professional person should be sought. *From a Declaration of Principles jointly adopted by a Committee of the American Bar Association and a Committee of Publishers.*

Library of Congress Cataloging-in-Publication Data

Crowther, Karmen N. T., 1942–
Researching your way to a good job / by Karmen N. T. Crowther.
p. cm.
Includes index.
ISBN 0-471-54824-3 (cloth : acid-free paper). — ISBN 0-471-54827-8 (paper : acid-free paper)
1. Job hunting—United States—Information services—Handbooks, manuals, etc. 2. Corporations—United States—Handbooks, manuals, etc. 3. Business enterprises—United States—Handbooks, manuals, etc. I. Title.
HF5382.75.U6C76 1993
650.14—dc20 92-9394

Printed in the United States of America

10 9 8 7 6 5 4 3 2 1

Preface

Getting a good job may seem a matter of luck—having the skills for the position advertised and being in the right place at the right time. As the vast majority of successful job seekers will tell you, however, luck played only a small part for them in obtaining the right job. Preparing a polished resume and cover letter took many hours and careful preparation helped them through their interviews. The key to their success in obtaining the right job, however, was *knowing the company.*

That's what this book is all about: researching a company to know about a prospective employer before you interview and even before you send out your resume. Once you know about a company, you hold a strong advantage. It is your qualifications, your ability, and your preparation (based on your knowledge of a company's needs and strengths), not luck, that will assure you of obtaining a good job.

Researching a prospective employer isn't something only beginners should do. It is an important job search technique that can be used successfully by seasoned professionals planning a job change as well as by first-time job seekers. As employment opportunities narrow in many fields and a growing number of companies restrict hiring plans, take the time to research and evaluate possible employers. It is a step that has valuable payoffs no matter what your previous experience or qualifications.

This book takes you through the company research process, beginning by identifying factors to investigate about prospective employers and by determining the ownership type of the company you are researching. You will find a discussion of well-known and widely available information sources useful for researching each type of company. Most of the sources recommended are available in medium-size public libraries or academic libraries. Suggestions are also included for other information contacts that you can access with a reasonable investment of time and effort.

Suggestions for locating information on special topics such as salaries, careers, or relocation are included, plus some additional tips for in-depth research possibilities. Finally, this book shows you how to use your company research findings in choosing prospective employers, writing a resume and cover letter, and performing well in an employment interview.

The more time and thoughtful consideration you devote to researching a prospective employer, the better your chances of finding the best possible position with a good employer. If the suggestions in this book can help you find the right job, we will have succeeded in our purpose.

My special thanks to the University of Tennessee, Knoxville Libraries and Dean Paula Kaufman for their generous extension of time and support to undertake this project. I want also to thank the UTK Career Services staff for proposing and supporting the initial presentation of these ideas; Martha Rudolph of the UTK Libraries for artwork; and my colleagues for their advice, suggestions, and encouragement. And, most of all, my thanks to Michael.

KARMEN N. T. CROWTHER
Strawberry Plains, Tennessee

Contents

PART III RESEARCHING SPECIAL TOPICS

PART IV USING COMPANY INFORMATION IN A JOB SEARCH

How to Use This Book

You don't need to read this book from cover to cover—though you might find it a good idea to do so. Rather, you can pick and choose the chapters or sections that are most useful to you and the type of company you want to research. Use the Contents and the chart on page viii–ix to decide where to begin.

If you are a novice to company research, start with Part I to discover the "who, why, and where" of investigating a prospective employer. Read the section called "Before You Begin: Advice from an Experienced Researcher"—it may improve your odds for successful company research. Part I also includes a survey of employer characteristics and a guide to company ownership types. Use these to determine the factors you want to explore and the type of company you are researching.

If you know the type of company you want to research (publicly owned, a subsidiary, privately held, foreign-owned, or small and local), go directly to the chapter in Part II discussing that company type. Use the Research Checklist at the beginning of each chapter in Part II as your guide to potential information sources.

Need some tips for researching salaries or a new location? Still thinking about your choice of careers? Want to explore *every* possibility in your company research? Part III has additional research tips for each of these areas.

Finally, look at Part IV for examples of how to use your company research in a job search. Employer selection, resumes and cover letters, interviews, and employment decisions are all reviewed, with ideas and examples for applying your company research to these segments.

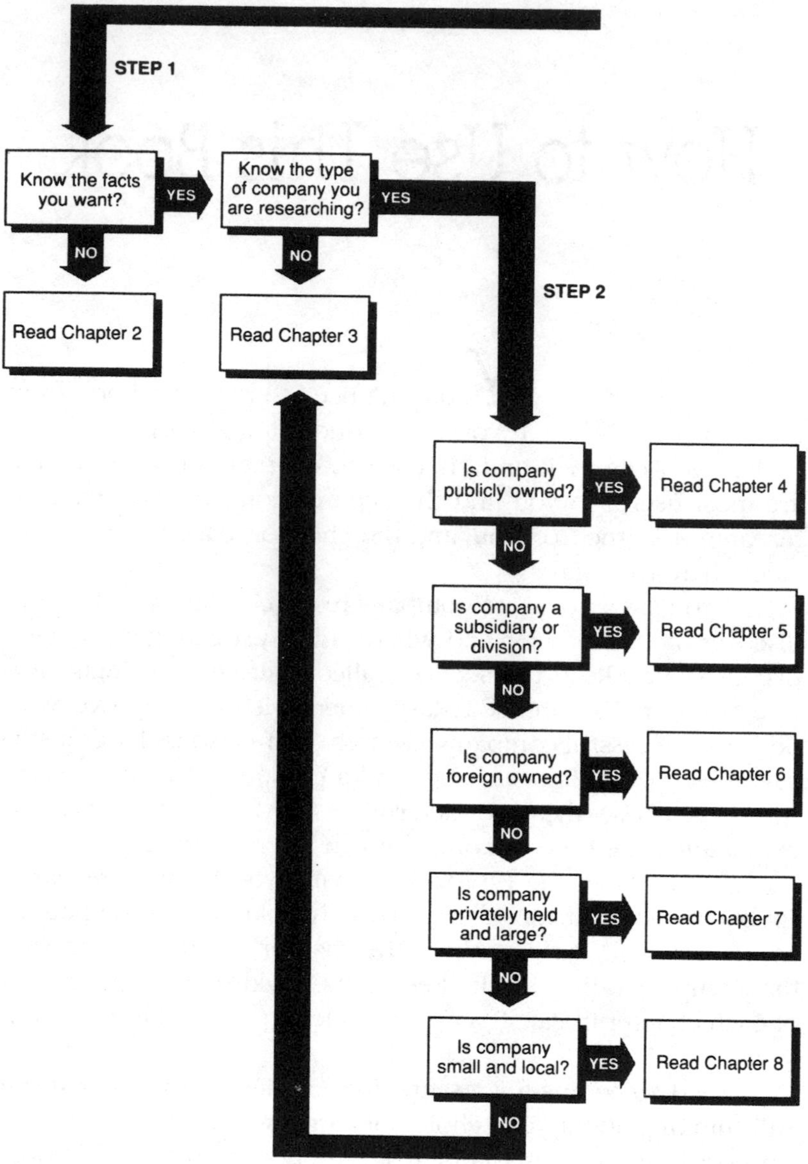
STEP 1
Know the facts you want?
YES
NO
Read Chapter 2
Know the type of company you are researching?
YES
NO
Read Chapter 3
STEP 2
Is company publicly owned?
YES
Read Chapter 4
NO
Is company a subsidiary or division?
YES
Read Chapter 5
NO
Is company foreign owned?
YES
Read Chapter 6
NO
Is company privately held and large?
YES
Read Chapter 7
NO
Is company small and local?
YES
Read Chapter 8
NO

How to use this book.

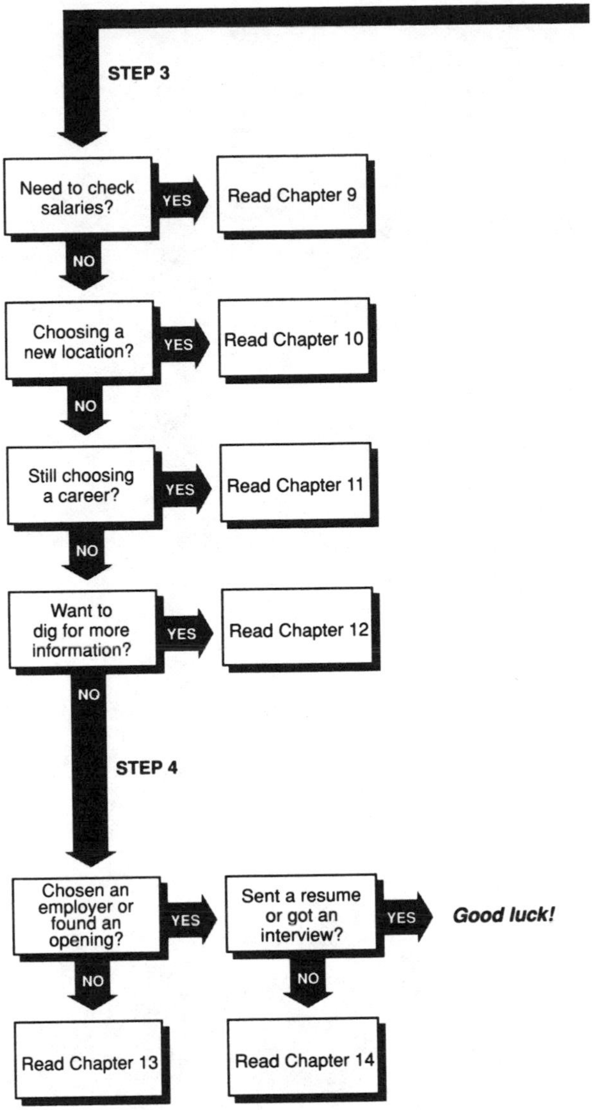

How to use this book. (Continued)

PART I

BEGINNING A JOB SEARCH

1 Why Research an Employer?

Chances are, when you send out your resume, when you go to an employment interview, and even when you accept a job offer, you know little about the organization that may become your employer. Perhaps you know the company's address and that it makes lawn mowers or computer chips, but do you know anything more? Do you know if the company is financially stable, has a reputation for quality products and service, or is interested in innovation? Does the company offer its employees opportunities for growth and promotion? Are long-term prospects for its industry good?

Imagine that you are choosing a new car. Would you be interested only in the color? Wouldn't you feel more confident about making a choice if you knew the car's sticker price and the possible resale or trade-in value? What about its estimated miles per gallon and repair record? If, like most people, you expect a car to give several years of enjoyment and service, you investigate the models that most interest you. Why not do the same when choosing an employer with whom you want to have several years of mutually rewarding affiliation?

How do you begin a search for a good employer? Most books for job seekers begin with advice about the resume and cover letter. These two documents typically serve as a company's first impression of an applicant. If the impression is a good one, an invitation to a job interview may follow. Job search experts often mention the importance of researching a company before going to an interview, maybe even before sending out the resume and cover letter. The advice, however, is usually brief enough to overlook. Can anything covered in only a page or two be as important as the resume or interview? The answer: *Yes, researching a company is important.* Learning about a prospective employer is basic to creating an appropriate resume and cover letter. It is fundamental to a successful interview and, most important, is central to establishing a mutually successful and enduring work relationship. Often overlooked, company research is the job search step this book will explore.

THE BENEFITS OF RESEARCHING A COMPANY

Most job hunters select potential employers haphazardly. They scan job advertisements in newspapers or professional publications and send out inquiries to any company that seeks someone with their qualifications. Others sign up for open interviews with any company whose recruiters are passing through their locality, or they canvas their friends and colleagues for leads. Still others send out dozens, even hundreds, of inquiry letters to a list of companies drawn from a telephone directory, hoping that their letter will reach a personnel officer's hands just as a vacancy occurs. In each of these scenarios, the job hunter knows little, if anything, about the companies that respond. The chances of being satisfied with an employer selected in this random way are poor. Although the fit between job hunter and employer may turn out well, the odds are slim. Still, job hunters use such hit-or-miss techniques again and again.

Help in Selecting Prospective Employers

What if you use a different approach? Instead of leaving the initial decision making to the employer, take the initiative into your own hands. Assemble a list of position vacancies and open interviews and then research each company using the methods described in this book. As you learn about a firm's organizational climate, its reputation and future outlook, its products and financial condition, you will have a better basis for judging whether you might be content working on its staff. If your research reveals major drawbacks in a prospective employer, you've saved the price of a first-class letter and possibly the time and disappointment of an unproductive interview. Alternatively, if your research turns up potential for a good match between a company's needs and prospects and your talents and aspirations, you have a chance for a successful interview.

If you plan to send out a number of blind inquiries, preliminary research will be even more effective. Don't send out resumes to every engineering firm in Chicago or all the advertising agencies in California. Apply a list of desired criteria to your company selection and you will create a more productive group of employment possibilities. Even if you consider only a firm's size or number of years in business, you will have made a start at evaluating characteristics that affect the company's current success and future viability. As you make your initial selections, you may also become aware that you have specific preferences about the kind of company you want to work for.

Better Cover Letters and Resumes

One of the benefits of research is that you begin to see how you might fit into a company and what you can offer to it. This is especially important as you begin preparing a cover letter and resume that will attract a company's attention and interest.

A good cover letter can establish your interest in the company and the position available, demonstrate the value you can bring to the organization, and highlight your strengths and abilities. If you can show in the first paragraph that you have a personal interest in the company or specific knowledge of its activity, it adds an individual touch that attracts the reader's attention. And, the more you know about the company, the better you can target your comments about your own qualifications.

You also can tailor your resume to a company's needs, based on your research. For example, suppose you have experience in both marketing and advertising and presently work in the food industry. You discover a promising job opening in marketing, but with a leading pharmaceutical company. Your research indicates that the firm has recently begun to diversify into new areas, primarily food additives and nutritional supplements; the food industry will be a major focus of the company's future marketing strategies. Based on these facts, highlight the relevant aspects of your background and experience in your resume, focusing on your marketing expertise and experience in the food industry—valuable attractions to this expanding firm.

More Effective Interviews

Researching a prospective employer can help in preparing a cover letter and resume that get the desired result—an interview. But how can your research affect the outcome of an interview? Based on what you learn, you will be able to respond to questions in a way that demonstrates the fit between your background and the company's needs.

Most books on job interviewing will suggest standard questions you should expect from the interviewer. Think through your answers to these questions. If you have studied the company, your answers will be on target, based on the skills and experience you offer and your knowledge of the firm's current operations and its outlook.

Often as the last step of an interview you will have an opportunity to ask questions. If you have done your homework, your research should reveal the key issues of interest or concern for any company you are considering as an employer. This is a good time to fill in unanswered gaps in your research and to find out anything the interviewer may have overlooked when briefing you.

Informed Employment Decisions

If things have gone well, the moment you hoped for arrives. You are offered a position and must decide whether to accept. Once again, your research will pay off. Your impressions gained during the interview will be important, but review all that you have learned about the firm and its industry. Consider what you discovered in your background research and the facts added during your interview. If your evaluation leaves you with a positive assessment of the company and the position offered, or with only a few unresolved and insignificant questions, go ahead. Accept the position and enjoy your new job!

WHICH JOB HUNTERS SHOULD RESEARCH PROSPECTIVE EMPLOYERS?

Perhaps you feel researching a prospective employer may be valuable for other job hunters, but you don't have time and you're already experienced in job hunting and interviewing. Think again! No matter what kind of job you are seeking, company research carries a big payoff.

First-Time Job Hunters

Are you a first-time job seeker with college graduation just around the corner? Do you have high expectations for your first job? Do you expect to stay with your employer for at least two or three years, gaining experience and training that will help you land another job with greater responsibility and higher pay after a few years? If the answer is yes to any of these questions, you need to find out enough about a first employer to ensure that you make the right choice for now as well as for the next few years. The adage that any job will do, just to gain experience, doesn't hold true in a highly competitive world. As you pursue your goals and ambitions, a wrong decision about a first employer may set you back or get you completely off track.

Experienced Job Hunters

Are you currently employed but want to move to another company? Do you want better pay, a promotion, greater challenges, more responsibility, or a change of scene? Would you prefer an employer whose goals and prospects are more compatible with your own? You may know all the pertinent information about a prospective employer if you are already employed in the industry—but you may not. You want to avoid making a change only to find that your new job is less satisfactory than your old one. Promotion and increased responsibility will mean little if a new employer's financial condition is precarious, its industry is scaling down, and layoffs—even bankruptcy—are possible. If you move to a new location seeking a better climate and surroundings, the sunny skies over a new home may darken if your new workplace is full of stress and bitter office politics. Spending a few hours on research to find out about a prospective employer can have long-term benefits in your personal job satisfaction.

Career Changers

Maybe you've experienced a mid-life crisis (actually, it can come along at any age) and want to try a new career. You're ready to give up a secure job for a new, but uncertain, tomorrow. You may have spent time and money acquiring new skills or polishing old ones and you want to ensure a successful new start. Should you trust to chance in choosing a new employer? Unless you want to find yourself in a dead end like the one you have just left, the answer is clearly no! Like a first-time job hunter, you are at the beginning of a career. Your choice will have a significant impact on your future satisfaction and success.

Reentry Job Hunters

Perhaps you are returning to the workplace after taking time off for advanced training or an additional degree. You may have spent some years at home raising a family or caring for an elderly parent. Perhaps you have taken advantage of part-time employment and now want to return full-time, to a new job with a different employer. Like other job hunters, you, too, need to learn all you can about prospective employers before interviewing or accepting a job offer.

You may feel at a disadvantage in job hunting because of your age or lack of recent experience. By thoroughly investigating possible employers, you acquire a marked advantage in a job search. You may also discover that your skills are exactly what a prospective employer needs, which will boost your confidence and be an asset in gaining an interview.

Recently Unemployed Job Hunters

If you are one of the growing number of those unemployed as a result of corporate downsizing, this is an opportunity to choose a new and, perhaps, better employer. The more time you spend researching a company's financial stability, its potential for growth and innovation, and its record of employee relations in periods of recession, the better your chances of a secure future. You may be tempted to accept your first job offer, particularly if additional openings appear limited and you are financially overextended. Even in that situation, company research can pay off. At least you will know and can anticipate any problems you may face with a less-than-perfect employer.

WHERE CAN YOU FIND THE INFORMATION YOU NEED?

Now that you are convinced company research is valuable to job-hunting success, how do you find out about a prospective employer? Many organizations collect information that may shed light on a company and its activities, but not all locations or resources are easily accessible. Start your research at the most convenient locations, but don't hesitate to explore other options.

What's Available to Students?

If you are a college student, you have a valuable advantage in researching prospective employers because campuses are filled with people dedicated to helping students make career choices. Your campus library has books and other materials containing company information; and reference librarians will guide you to the best places to start your research. Your teachers and advisors may be familiar with companies through community contacts or their research. Many faculty members have special insights as a result of consulting for a company or industry. Don't hesitate to ask for their advice.

Every campus has a placement or career guidance center to assist students seeking employment after graduation. In addition to serving as an interviewing and credentials center for company recruiters visiting campuses, many placement centers maintain a collection of materials about prospective employers. Companies often send pamphlets and reports to placement centers for the use of students interested in employment. If you have not yet decided on a career, the placement service can also help you evaluate your interests and abilities.

What's Available to Alumni?

Most colleges and universities provide their alumni with limited access to campus services. Placement services are almost always available to former students, including access to career and employer information materials. College and university libraries, particularly those of publicly supported institutions, are often open to former students and to the general public. Although borrowing may be restricted, you may usually use materials in the building and seek assistance from the librarians.

What's Available to the Currently Employed?

If you are employed when you start a job search, you, too, have certain advantages when researching a new employer, particularly if you expect to stay in the same industry. Large companies often have their own corporate libraries with a wealth of specialized material on other companies in the same industry. After a few years on the job, you may have a network of contacts working within your industry, or even for your prospective employer, who can answer questions. You may also belong to a professional association that provides job placement assistance as well as opportunities to meet others employed in your field. Now is the perfect time to put that network of colleagues you have established to work for you, gathering information on a prospective job opportunity and new employer.

What's Available to the Currently Unemployed?

No longer a student and not currently employed? Where should you begin to hunt for information on prospective employers? The public library would be an excellent choice; you will find answers there to many of your initial questions. Locating answers to any remaining questions might depend on the companies you are researching. Civic associations and government offices are only two possibilities; many others also exist. And you, too, may have a network of trusted friends, former employers, and others who can help you find information about a company.

BEFORE YOU BEGIN: ADVICE FROM AN EXPERIENCED RESEARCHER

Before you begin searching for information about a prospective employer, stop for these words of advice. They may make your research easier and your expectations of results more realistic.

1. Begin your research at a library or information center. You will save time by surveying the available published materials first. They provide background data that will enable you to search more efficiently for additional information in other locations.

2. No single location may have everything you need. For example, if you begin at a college or university library, also visit the public library or search out special resource centers, particularly corporate libraries with materials on specific industries. Each location may have different materials available.

3. Explain the purpose of your research to the librarian and ask for suggestions. Trained in information-seeking skills, a librarian can provide professional advice and assistance by suggesting specific items of research value.

4. If you want a full profile of a prospective employer, look beyond your library. Local, state, and federal government offices, for example, routinely gather data about companies and industries for statistical and regulatory purposes. Many civic and professional organizations have strong ties to the business community. News organizations, financial institutions, competitors, suppliers—all are possibilities. It is not always

convenient or easy to gain access to these sources, however. Try to schedule your contacts after completing your preliminary research. In that way, you will have a clearer idea of what you are seeking and may be more successful in requesting information.

5. Set priorities before you start. Rank the factors about a prospective employer that are most important to you, and rank, also, the most potentially revealing topics about a company. Because you may not find all the information you seek, spend your time where it will have greatest impact.

6. Always take thorough notes—first-rate advice no matter how often you hear it. That important fact you are sure you will remember is the first one you will forget. It also is wise to write down where you found a particular item of information if you need to go back later and confirm your notes. Note also the names of people who assist you. If you must call back or return for a second visit, you may want to ask for them again.

7. Devise a form or outline if you intend to research several companies. Fill in facts in each category of the outline as you find them, noting their source, and you will see at a glance what you still have to locate for each company. The sample form included here (Figure 1.1) suggests a research outline.

8. Published information may be rather dated (from several months to several years old) depending on the current level of interest in a subject, requirements for making data available to the public, or the time it takes to get materials into print and into libraries and bookstores. Always check the date of publication of any materials you use.

9. Be alert to the authority of your information sources. If you are using a book, read the Introduction or the "Guide to Users" to find out how the author obtained the information. Never regard any printed source as infallible. No matter how qualified, all authors and publishers make occasional errors and omissions.

Company ______________________ Telephone Number ______________

Address ______________________ Personnel Officer ______________

Position Available ______________ Where Listed ______________

Send Resume? Yes ☐ No ☐ Date ______________

SUBJECT	FINDINGS	SOURCE
1. Location		
2. Facilities		
3. Size		
4. Product/Service		
5. Financial Data		
6. Company Strategies/Goals		
7. Response to Difficulty		
8. Management/Employee Data		
9. Executive Biography		
10. Employee Morale		
11. Salaries		
12. Industry Outlook		

Figure 1.1 Company research form.

10. Information on very recent developments (the past four to six weeks) can be difficult to locate unless you are willing to browse through recent issues of newspapers and magazines or have access to an electronic information service updated on a daily basis. It takes several weeks or months for articles to be indexed and for indexes to be published and available.

11. Business information in electronic format has expanded rapidly in the past decade. Many highly specialized and previously restricted materials have gained far wider distribution through this medium. Electronic access is fast, the data is timely and specific, and the systems are flexible and often cost-effective. Don't overlook this option.

12. You may find it helpful, as you research a company, to compare it with others in the same industry. Choose a company that is widely respected and highly praised and analyze it for similar factors. This will provide a standard of comparison for any prospective employer in the industry.

13. Everything you want to know about a company is ***not*** written down, published, and readily available. This is particularly true for small firms and privately held companies, but it also holds for some large public corporations. In some instances, personal contacts or informed observers may be able to provide answers or opinions. Despite your best efforts, however, some questions may remain unanswered.

14. You can't start your research the hour before your interview and expect to learn anything that will improve your chances of getting the perfect job. Chances are, however, you won't begin investigating a company weeks ahead of time. Therefore, you must decide how much time to devote to your research, knowing that there will be a direct ratio between the time you spend and the amount and usefulness of the information you locate.

Good luck as you start your search for the perfect employer!

2 Selecting Company Factors to Investigate

What factors are important in evaluating a company or organization as a prospective employer? What characteristics will best define the perfect employer for you? A standard group of categories can be identified, regardless of the job opening or career field you are considering, but the answers may vary widely. Performance that is adequate or outstanding for one company may, because of industry circumstances or economic conditions, appear substandard or lacking for another. Achievements you rate as satisfactory in a prospective employer may be disappointing to someone else.

The suggestions in this chapter are guidelines—factors, questions, and issues for you to consider as you research any company. You may not need or be able to find evidence in every category suggested in this chapter. On the other hand, questions specific only to the company you are studying may also have a bearing on whether that firm will be a good employer for you. You must decide the questions that need answers and the information that is relevant, perhaps even critical, to your appraisal. Finally, based on the results of your research, you must evaluate whether a company might be a good employer for you.

The second section of this book, Part II, contains suggestions of specific sources and methods for locating the answers to the factors outlined here, depending on the type of company you are researching. Refer back to "How to Use This Book" on page vii when you have selected the factors that you want to research (or any others that are important to you) and you are ready to begin.

LOCATION

Often, the first question job seekers ask about a prospective employer is, "Where is the company located?" An address may be one of the easiest pieces of information to find, but location is a broader issue than just a company's address. Does the company do business in only one location, or does it have divisions or subsidiaries located in many cities or even in foreign countries? Does it have more than one location within a city? At what location, exactly, is the job opening you are considering? If the company has several locations, are employees transferred among them? How frequently?

How important is geographical location to you? If a company is in a different region from where you now live, are you willing to relocate? If relocation is acceptable, are certain geographical factors important to you? Do you prefer a cold, snowy location with proximity to ski areas so that you can enjoy winter sports? Do you prefer a dry, pollen-free climate for health reasons? Do you want to live in an urban or rural location? Are you interested in working in a company's foreign offices?

FACILITIES

You may also want to consider the size and age of a company's facilities. Are the buildings and grounds well maintained? If the buildings are old, have they been modernized or renovated, or are there plans to do so? If your interview takes place off site, you may need to ask about the facility in the location where you would be working. Although some companies take pride in maintaining an attractive facility that contributes to the organization's public image, other companies choose not to invest in their physical facility or believe its appearance and condition are unrelated to the effective functioning of the organization. You will want to consider which environment is more comfortable for you.

COMPANY SIZE

Many people have strong preferences about working for a large or a small organization. Working for a large company may have advantages, for you can learn by observing more experienced co-workers. Large companies may offer higher salaries and more extensive benefits, along with a greater variety of opportunities. In a large company, however, it may take longer for a new employee to attain significant responsibilities or receive a promotion. A small company may offer hands-on experience and more immediate impact on activities and planning. Opportunities for peer and mentoring relationships may be few, however, and paths to advancement may be limited.

You can measure a company's size in several ways. Number of employees is an easy factor to determine and is often used as a standard of size. But always weigh additional factors such as productivity or labor intensiveness for a balanced view of employee numbers. A manufacturer, for example, may require a larger labor force than its competitors if its processes are not automated. A hotel or resort may require a large staff if a high standard of personal service is a priority. Keep in mind that employee numbers measure size, not success.

Financial size, as measured by annual sales, is also a quick standard of comparison between companies. Often an easy factor to discover, sales can reveal comparative span and strength of companies within the same industry. As with employee numbers, however, it is easy to place too much emphasis on isolated figures. Ideally, you should review total annual sales along with other financial data such as inventory, overhead, or long-term debt. For example, annual sales of $15 billion may mean financial losses and layoffs for one auto manufacturer, while sales of only $5 billion could produce a record year and employee bonuses for another. Even within the same industry, annual sales alone is not an indicator of success.

Comparisons of annual sales figures are difficult when reviewing companies in different industries. Annual sales of two high-tech surveillance satellites by a company employing 10 engineers and technicians, for example, may equal the total dollar sales of 3 million thermos bottles by a firm employing 500 assembly workers. You must consider additional data to accurately measure company size across industries.

If size in employee numbers or annual sales is difficult to determine, investigate other factors relating to size. You can compare architectural or construction firms by the number of contracts bid or completed; you can evaluate manufacturers by the number of product units produced or sold; and you can assess service organizations, ranging from hotels to museums to churches, by the number of clients or users served. In some cases, the physical size of a company's facilities or resources (miles of railroad track, acres of forest, square feet of production space) may be a factor in appraising its viability.

PRODUCT AND/OR SERVICE

Never send a resume or go to an interview without knowing a company's product or service. This is essential information for a job seeker. You won't impress an interviewer favorably if you haven't bothered to learn this fundamental fact before you arrive for your appointment. When the position is with a corporate division or subsidiary, know the products that part of the company is responsible for. If you are unsure which division of a multifaceted company you might be assigned to, find out *all* the company's lines of business. No one will expect you to know details, but be familiar with the company's general industry concentrations. The more you know, the better you can target your resume and your interview responses.

The following factors are related to a company's product or service: retail prices for the company's products; the products that are the firm's chief money earners and their sales volume; the company's share of the total market for the products; the quality of the products as compared with the competition; and the importance of technology to the products. These are useful facts to know, but answers are not always publicly available. If you locate this data, it will expand your picture of a company and its products. If you do not, these are good questions to ask during an interview.

Don't overlook a company's chief competitors, both at home and abroad. Knowing who they are can help you understand the field a company plays on. Consider, also, a company's major customers and their geographic concentration, if any. Whenever possible, observe how a company markets or advertises its products and whether it does so effectively. How much money is budgeted for this effort? Again, answers to these questions may be difficult to find. Depending on the position you are seeking and the type of company you are studying, allocate your research time accordingly.

FINANCIAL DATA

Financial data are probably, after an address, the most commonly sought company information. Every company researcher—and job hunters are no exception—gives this a high priority. Although financial data are important in assessing a company's current economic status and its long-term prospects, such information can be easy to locate or very difficult, depending on the company's ownership type. Chapter 3 will outline how ownership is the key to finding information. But first, what financial indicators are most useful in evaluating a prospective employer?

One quick financial indicator is whether a company is making a profit. Profit is defined as sales minus costs and expenses. Many good companies may have legitimate reasons for not making a profit. Start-up companies frequently take several years to show a profit. If they have recently undertaken a major expansion or fought off a takeover bid, established companies may not show a profit for several years. The important question in all cases is: Are profits expected? When?

Annual sales not only is a factor in evaluating company size but is also central to analyzing financial stability and growth. Have sales steadily increased? What is the ratio of sales to employees? Is it comparable to other firms in the industry? If a company has several divisions, what are the sales of the division you hope to interview with? If you cannot determine the exact dollar amount, then what is its percentage of total corporate sales? Don't be surprised if you have trouble locating specific data because often it is not publicly available.

In addition to investigating profits and sales, look at the reverse side of the financial picture—costs and liabilities. Costs are the day-to-day expenses of doing business: supplies, salaries, rents, taxes, overhead, and so on. Liability usually refers to short- or long-term debts such as loans and mortgages. Every company will have debts and obligations, for they are a routine part of conducting business. They become a problem only when they exceed a company's ability to recover from them. For perspective when evaluating this factor, consider a company's debt status over a period of at least three to five years. Also, compare its debt status with others in the same industry.

Consider the price of a publicly owned company's stocks or bonds. The price is often a good measure of public confidence in a company. Take care in evaluating price fluctuations, however, because a declining stock value may be a response to a widespread economic downturn affecting the entire stock market. A rising value could reflect unwarranted speculation not related to the actual viability and worth of a company.

As you look at the financial information you are able to locate, review several years of activity to get perspective on a company's long-term outlook. Every company has good and bad years. Try to determine the cause of any unusual fluctuations, and whether they might recur with negative results for the company. Look, too, at industry norms when assessing the company.

In addition to specific financial data, what is the company's overall financial condition? Does it appear stable? Would the company be categorized as a fiscally conservative firm or as a risk taker? Is it an attractive takeover candidate? If yes, a takeover could lead, on the plus side, to more available capital, increased opportunity for expansion, and more rapid advancement of capable staff, opening up positions for new employees like you. On the minus side, it could mean reduced operating funds, restricted growth, and staff firings, especially of newly hired employees (again, like you) as a new management team takes over.

If the company is a large corporation with several subsidiaries and divisions, note whether these are regularly acquired and sold off. In a process called "asset stripping," some corporations routinely purchase companies, gut them of their financial value and best staff, and then sell them again. On the other hand, ailing companies are sometimes purchased at a bargain price. The acquiring firm brings in new management, revitalizing the staff and accomplishing a rapid and dramatic financial turnaround. The company, now a valuable asset, may be quickly sold again at a substantial profit.

A word of caution about financial data: Figures can be misleading if you have only partial data as well as confusing if you are unfamiliar with financial reports. If you feel that your evaluation of a prospective employer requires a full analysis of a company's financial status, you may need to detour at this point to learn how to interpret financial statements. A broker, financial advisor, or banker may be able to provide a simple explanation of basic financial analysis. Help is also available at your library, where you can find both book-length studies and pamphlets explaining financial statements. The following source, for example, briefly describes and explains corporate financial data:

The Business One–Irwin Business and Investment Almanac. Business One–Irwin. Annual.

> This handbook of business and financial information contains a brief section, "How to Understand and Analyze Financial Statements," that explains what to look for when reading a company's financial report and what the data means. Check the *Almanac's* index under "Financial Statements" for the relevant pages.

COMPANY HISTORY

The company history available for the firm you are researching may vary from a full-length book to only a sentence or two. The first option is more than you want to know, the second not enough. At a minimum, find out when the company was founded, any significant events in its past, and any major changes of purpose or organization that have occurred. You need not be an expert on an organization's past, but it is useful to know something of the ethos that formed the company.

When researching company history keep these cautions in mind: First, age alone is not a indicator of a company's prospects. In difficult financial times, an old, established firm is as likely to face bankruptcy, takeover, or severe cutbacks as a young one. Nor does a history of less than five years indicate that a company's long-term outlook is precarious. While all entrepreneurial firms present some risks for an employee, every established, successful firm was once young and entrepreneurial. Age sometimes indicates a conservative corporate outlook. Marketplace pressures and management changes make that adage less true than it once was, however.

Don't overlook the role that founding families may continue to play in an organization. Do they control the board of directors or the choice of top managers in the company? Are they feuding—either with one another or the current company management?

Finally, identify the source of any company history. A company may commission the writing of its own history. Such histories are rather common and are generally very positive in outlook. They frequently become the source for subsequent versions of a company's past and, while the picture presented may not be deliberately false, it may be incomplete. Look for a second, independent version if the history seems too rosy.

COMPANY STRATEGIES AND GOALS

The current strategies and the long-term goals of a company are often difficult for an outsider to discern. Few companies make such plans public, certainly not in any detail. It is possible, however, to find clues about where a company is headed and how it expects to get there. Look back at the company's activities over the past three to five years and look for a consistent pattern of corporate behavior. Such patterns provide an indication, even without written confirmation, of the company's immediate strategies and long-term goals. Unless there is a major management shake-up or unexpected economic decline in the next few years, responses may continue in a similar pattern for the near future.

Other questions to consider might include, for example, the company's record on innovation. Does the company support new research to strengthen or broaden its product lines? Research and development spending is one clue to this, as is the number of staff allocated to research tasks. Some companies support university research projects or fund venture opportunities for new companies in the hope of acquiring successful new technologies through their corporate sponsorship. If you can discover the company's areas of research interest, you may be able to guess the new markets it expects to enter.

The competitive status of most companies demands active programs to match and surpass their competitors. Tangible evidence of such efforts is often corporate commitment to service and to quality. The success of such programs, however, demands the active support and participation of all company employees. Does the company you are researching have such programs? Can you gauge if the commitment to quality and service goes beyond lip service?

A company's response to innovation and competition may also indicate its openness to new ideas in all aspects of the firm's operation. Has the company ever been an industry leader? Can you identify any project in which it has taken the initiative? What has been the payback to the company of such projects? How do they fit the goals of the organization?

How has the company responded to changes in the economy? What was its financial strategy in times of easy credit and in periods of economic downturn? How has it treated employees in terms of continued employment, retraining, or salaries and benefits? With the current trend toward downsizing in American business, this factor merits careful consideration.

RESPONSE TO DIFFICULTY

Companies, like individuals, meet with difficulties of every kind and dimension during their existence. Most problems will be handled quickly and with little fanfare. A few, however, may grow into major dilemmas encompassing scandal, financial reversal, government investigation, public outcry over products or policies, or employee litigation. Your primary concern is how a company responds to its problems.

Examine first of all, what a company has done to ameliorate any difficult situation. What was the immediate response to the crisis? How effective was it? Who was responsible for framing the response—the company management or outside hired consultants? If the immediate response was merely a stopgap solution, what was the long-term resolution? Was this the only such difficulty the company faced or merely one of a string of repeated problems? If the problem recurred, does the company appear to have modified the procedures or activities that precipitated it? Were there internal changes in management strategy or personnel as a result? Finally, is the company financially stable and successful in all other respects?

Even highly regarded companies may find themselves inadvertently in difficulty, and the business literature is full of such cases. A classic example is the Tylenol tampering case of the early 1980s. Seven Chicago area deaths resulted from the ingestion of Tylenol capsules deliberately tainted with cyanide. Tylenol's manufacturer, Johnson & Johnson, moved quickly to restore public confidence in their product, pulling all the capsules from stores. Reintroduced in tamper-proof packaging, Tylenol sales soon rebounded and the company emerged relatively unscathed from the incident. Not all companies are so successful in stemming public concern. The Alaska oil spill of the *Exxon Valdez* in 1989 continues to arouse public criticism, despite Exxon's large cleanup effort and landmark fine payment.

Still other companies face problems because activities and procedures once widely practiced are retroactively judged unacceptable. Public health concerns over smoking, for example, have aroused significant negative public opinion about the tobacco industry. Companies producing tobacco products have also faced several legal challenges in recent years. As you look at such incidents, the key factor to consider in evaluating a prospective employer is how the company has recovered or responded to its difficulty.

MANAGEMENT AND EMPLOYEE DATA

Employee numbers were noted earlier as a measure of company size. You can use other employee and management data to answer additional questions. If you can locate a breakdown of the company's employees by assignment or department, it may indicate the activities valued or stressed within the corporation. For example, a high proportion of employees assigned to research and development activity might indicate a company concerned with staying on the cutting edge of technological developments. A large human resources staff might indicate concern for employee welfare or, instead, problems with employee morale and retention.

Determine, if you can, the number of employees classed as management, white-collar, or blue-collar workers. Is the proportion representative of other companies in the industry? If not, what reason can you discern for the difference? The ratio might reveal an organization with too much bureaucracy. Alternatively, it could reflect a highly automated workplace with reduced need for clerical or manual labor. Is the current ratio an asset to the company; can they sustain it?

How is the company's management team organized? Ideally, you would examine an organization chart. Chances are, you won't see one of these until after you are hired—and sometimes not even then. However, if you can discover how management is deployed, you may gain valuable clues about the organization's power structure. It might also reveal some unusual reporting relationships—indicators that a management overhaul is needed or, maybe, that an innovative organization structure is being explored.

What about the nonmanagement work force? A big question here is whether it is unionized. Although unions are on the defensive in the United States with membership falling and the number of local right-to-work laws increasing, a large number of American workers are still union members. If you are considering a unionized company, find out what unions are present. What is the general quality of union–management relations in the company? When is the union contract next up for renegotiation? What is the likely outcome?

In some industries, strikes can have devastating financial effects for all employees, even forcing companies into bankruptcy. Crossing picket lines during a strike is uncomfortable and can be dangerous for employees at any level, not just the "scabs" brought in to replace strikers. Even in normal working conditions, dealing with union work rules can be troublesome; but anyone in a supervisory position must understand and heed these rules—not just top management and human resources staff.

White-collar workers, especially those who work for state and local government and those in public education, may be unionized. As an entry-level employee, you might find yourself faced with the necessity to join a union. For some individuals, this is a difficult and unpalatable choice, while others view it as an affirmation of the working heritage of our nation. Whatever your decision, the key to a good workplace is the relationship between the union and the employer. In the best circumstances, it should reflect mutual respect and concern for the continued strength and viability of the organization.

EXECUTIVE BIOGRAPHY

Knowledge of a company's top management is not essential, but it is one more piece to add to the picture you are developing of a prospective employer. As a rule, only those in the top positions of the nation's major corporations are well-known outside their own firms or their own locality. Don't be surprised if you have trouble tracking down the executives of smaller companies or the middle managers of larger firms.

The primary benefit of biographical data about an employer is that it can provide clues to the training and experience valued by the company. For example, if most of the top executives of an auto parts manufacturer were trained as engineers or have completed advanced management study at an Ivy League college, an undergraduate business degree from a midwestern university might limit a person's chances for advancement to the top ranks in the company. If every manager in a company has risen from the ranks and been with the firm for more than 30 years, you have two clues about the organization: It is possible to advance within the company; and younger managers, and those with viewpoints shaped by experience gained outside the company, may have a long wait for a turn at the top. If this is your first job or the fast track has little appeal for you, such information may not seem important. If you are ambitious, however, and have high aspirations, spend some time studying the executives who might become your colleagues.

At a minimum, find out the names of the chairman of the board and the chief executive officer or president of a company. You will want to recognize their names if you hear them. You almost certainly won't be meeting them at an interview, unless the company is very small or prides itself on an extremely collegial atmosphere—or unless you are seeking a high-level management position yourself. By the way, if any of the company executives just happen to be family friends, it is usually better to let the interviewer bring up their names first.

If you're not seeking a top management position, spend your time learning about the middle managers. These are the people you are most likely to have contact with if hired, and you may profit from knowing their background. Middle managers, however, are almost anonymous. Facts about them rarely, if ever, appear in published sources. Your best chance of learning about these individuals may depend on whether you have personal contacts within the company or industry.

Don't overlook, by the way, the nonworkplace interests of a company's executives. You might find that several of a firm's executives are on the boards of local arts organizations. Before sending a resume to that company, add to it, if appropriate, your participation in community theater, amateur opera productions, or other applicable activity. That small personal connection might just be the deciding factor in setting your resume apart from dozens of others with similar qualifications.

EMPLOYEE MORALE

Employees' feelings about their work and their employer are difficult to gauge. Although current employees can provide the best answers, you may not have such contacts. If you do, remember that one person's opinion seldom gives a well-rounded picture of the atmosphere within a company. Try to get several opinions and balance them with additional information. Remember, too, that praise or complaints based on the situation a year or more ago may now be invalid in the face of management change or financial crisis.

Whether or not you have an inside contact, questions based on fact rather than opinion are the best starting places.

For example, do employees have a high turnover rate? If so, is the turnover primarily in one department or division? If the turnover is not in the department where you will be working, it may not affect your work or your attitudes about the company. If the turnover is general, however, can you determine the cause? Although companies sometimes go through major restructuring, with a peak number of retirements and furloughs, the changes may be ultimately beneficial to the organization and not indicative of an ongoing internal problem.

What is the company's past record on human relations? Have there been proven cases of racial discrimination, sexism, or wage inequities? Are programs for employee support in place? In addition to the usual benefits, are there provisions in the company rules for employee drug and alcohol treatment programs, parental as well as maternity leave, child care assistance, and so on? If there have been layoffs in the company's past, what is its record in assisting workers to find other employment?

Other questions about employee morale will be more difficult to answer, as they may be based on emotional responses rather than facts. For example: Are employees sure of their role in the organization? Are they confident of their employer's expectations of them in accomplishing the organization's goals? Are projects clearly defined and are staff effectively assigned? Does the firm encourage and listen to employee suggestions? Do people feel adequately rewarded for their work, not only in monetary terms, but in recognition and appreciation? What is the political environment in the workplace? Does internal feuding inhibit productivity? Can you sense an atmosphere of malaise or of optimism among employees?

If you are unable to gauge employee morale fully before you contact the company or before you have an interview, keep these questions in mind. Should the company be interested in you and arrange an interview, try to get a sense of the firm's atmosphere as you talk to the interviewer and other staff you encounter. Their relationships with one another as well as their questions and comments to you may indicate how employees function within the company, both as individuals and as a group. If possible, ask questions of your own to assess employees' attitudes about their employer.

Ultimately you may have to judge employee satisfaction within a company solely on your emotional response. Although it is always best to base career decisions on tangible factors, at some level you must decide if you feel comfortable with the company, its people, and its atmosphere. Do your best to find hard facts; then use your own best judgment in evaluating the company's morale.

SALARIES

The salary scale for entry level positions is generally quoted in a job advertisement. Positions requiring previous experience often suggest a minimum salary level or ask the applicant to state a salary history or requirement. No matter what position you seek, salary questions are a part of company research.

First, is the pay scale quoted by the company reasonable for the training and level of experience sought? Compare the suggested salary with that of similar positions advertised by other companies during the past 6 to 12 months. Do the company's salary scales match those that ask for similar qualifications? Is the salary commensurate with others in the same industry? An electrical engineer working for a public utility, for example, may not claim the same salary as an equally experienced engineer at an electronics firm, but should expect to match others working in his or her particular specialty.

Look also at salaries for positions you hope to qualify for in a few years. Compare that salary with the one you might command today to get a rough idea of salary increases you might expect from an employer over time. What are local pay scales? Keep in mind that the cost of living in large urban areas frequently inflates salaries so that not all localities will meet nationally quoted salary minimums for similar positions. However, salaries in the company you are researching should be comparable to other employers in its area. Demand is also a factor in salary levels. Can you measure the current or future demand for your career field or speciality? An overcrowded field with many potential job candidates will mean lower salaries.

Has the company in question gained a reputation for its salaries? Even small companies may have an industrywide, or even nationwide, reputation for rewarding their employees handsomely. Other firms may be known for offering high starting salaries but seldom extending raises thereafter. Still others may offer notoriously low salaries but remain attractive as prospective employers because they offer a stimulating, creative atmosphere or the opportunity to work with the leaders in a particular field.

Don't forget to consider the extras provided by some companies in addition to the package of standard benefits: vacation, sick leave, insurance, and retirement. Look for the unusual. Are there employee stock purchase options, tax-sheltered savings plans, educational leave with pay, management training programs, use of company-owned vacation facilities, parental leave, in-house child care facilities, or financial assistance to dependents for college education? Some of these extras add significant additional value to the salary offered.

INDUSTRY OUTLOOK

To have a full picture of a prospective employer, you must also look at the industry it competes in. Look, too, at the general economic conditions in which a company operates and how it responds to them.

Start with the industry's competitive status. If it is facing tough foreign or domestic competition and has done so for several years, companies in that field are likely to be leaner and meaner than those in industries with little competition. Firms that have endured through difficult times will have adopted responses that ensure their continued survival and are likely to stress these factors in future ventures. Such factors may enhance the company's standing as a good employer. Alternatively, if an industry is only beginning to see signs of tough times ahead, you must judge whether the company you are considering as an employer will be among those that can adapt and survive. Based on past actions, does this particular company have the will to change so that it can remain among the leaders and survivors of its industry? Is the company likely to try playing it safe in a bid for time or other mitigating factors?

Seek out both a short-term and a long-term analysis of what the future may hold for the industry. To accept a job with a company in an industry undergoing a brief decline may not be a mistake if an upturn is likely in the near future. On the other hand, joining a firm in an industry whose long-term prospects are bleak is probably not a good idea, unless you are convinced the company can turn the situation around and be a survivor.

Look, too, at the possibility of increased foreign competition. Competition from East Asia in the past decade has already had significant impact on U.S. industry. The economic integration of Europe and a North American free trade agreement will also influence the American market. Finally, don't overlook the past record or future possibility of government regulation and how this affects an industry's viability.

What is an industry's leverage on its own situation? Is it well organized? Does it have an active trade or professional association that works to promote its products and services? Does the association attempt to influence public policy locally or nationally in support of its interests? Does it have an energetic educational and public relations arm? In addition to industrywide support efforts, some associations provide member companies with information services, technical assistance, statistical data, an employment clearinghouse, newsletters, and a variety of additional services for individuals.

From the preceding suggestions and from personal factors that are important to you, draw up a list of factors to investigate about prospective employers. Don't forget that your final evaluation of an employer should depend on your background, skills, and ambitions as well as the circumstances of the firm you are researching. If you know the type of company, based on its ownership, that you are considering, begin exploring the information sources in Part II. If not, read the next chapter for help in determining a company's ownership status.

3 Identifying the Type of Company You Want to Research

A company's form of ownership generally determines the type and amount of information that is publicly available and easily accessible. Your key, then, to company research is to determine the firm's ownership type. Is it a publicly owned or privately held corporation? Is it a subsidiary or a division of another firm? Is it foreign owned? Is it a local or regional company with a limited market or outlook? If you are unsure what is meant by a company's type of ownership, the following sections briefly outline company organization types.

COMPANY OWNERSHIP

Although a variety of business ownership forms are possible, the primary ones are the sole proprietorship, the partnership, and the corporation. The sole proprietorship is owned by one person, who has full managerial power and the right to all profits but also assumes personal liability for all company losses. In a partnership, two or more persons contract to carry on business together. The partners share the same powers, rights, and personal liabilities as the sole proprietor but pool their resources and efforts. Neither a sole proprietorship nor a partnership lasts beyond the lifetime of its owners. Few of the companies you want to research will fall into either of these categories, for sole proprietorships and partnerships are generally small, local companies with limited scope.

Your primary interest will be in the corporation—a company formed through the process of incorporation. By incorporating, a company becomes a kind of artificial person, legally authorized to carry on a business enterprise. Ownership of the corporation is represented by its capital stock, the money invested in the firm. The stock is divided into shares, and control of the corporation is vested in those who own shares—the stockholders. The stockholders share in all profits but have limited personal liability for the corporation's losses. As stock can be transferred among shareholders, the corporation has an unlimited life.

Publicly Owned and Privately Held Corporations

Corporations generally fall into two categories: publicly owned corporations and privately or closely held corporations. A publicly owned enterprise seeks investment by selling shares in its stock to the public on a stock exchange or through "over-the-counter" markets. These "publicly" owned corporations are required by law to file financial disclosure statements with the U.S. Securities and Exchange Commission (SEC) in Washington, D.C. A public corporation must also submit to its stockholders an annual report of its financial condition. These documents contain both financial and management information about the corporation that becomes widely available in many additional forms, including a variety of resources found in libraries and information centers.

A privately owned corporation, in contrast, retains its shares of stock among a limited group of individuals. Because it does not seek capital investment from outsiders and does not offer its shares to the public, it need not report its financial condition to the SEC. Only the corporation's small group of investors are fully aware of its financial standing. As a consequence, information about privately held corporations, especially financial information, can be difficult to find. Published sources found in libraries have only limited information about privately held corporations.

The difference between a publicly owned and a privately owned firm is a key factor that will influence any company research. Because publicly owned corporations sell shares of their stock to the general public, they must report their financial condition to their stockholders and to the federal government; thus, the public at large has access to this information. Private corporations do not publicly trade their stock and, therefore, are not required to disclose their financial status. Such information is generally confidential.

Subsidiaries and Divisions

A business firm, whether public or private, may come to dominate another corporation through the ownership or control of its stock. A common method of establishing control is a merger or takeover through stock purchase. The dominant corporation in such circumstances is known as the "parent" company. When the parent owns the majority or all of the stock of another firm, that firm is known as its subsidiary. The subsidiary, however, remains a separately chartered firm and in some complex corporate structures may even continue to have its own subsidiaries. The stock shares of the subsidiary are generally exchanged for shares in the parent and stock is no longer publicly traded in the subsidiary's name.

The division is another common form of organizational control. A corporation may set up a separate branch or "division" to produce or manage a group of product lines or services. The division is closely integrated with the parent but, unlike a subsidiary, is not a separately chartered business. Stock shares may be purchased only in the name of the parent corporation, not its divisions.

If you determine that a company is a subsidiary or division, how will it affect your search for information? Although a publicly owned corporation must file financial disclosure reports with the U.S. Securities and Exchange Commission, the SEC requires detailed reporting only on the corporation as a unified entity. A single report in the parent corporation's name represents the entire organization, with only minimal data being required for its subsidiaries and divisions. The corporation's annual report to its stockholders also represents the total corporate condition and provides less full description and accounting for its individual corporate segments.

Privately held corporations may also have subsidiaries and divisions. Just as with business segments of publicly owned corporations, less information may be available for the subsidiaries and divisions of a privately held corporation than for their parent. Additional information access problems are posed by the confidentiality practices of private ownership.

Foreign-Owned Companies

A growing number of foreign companies are purchasing controlling interest in U.S. firms or establishing branch locations in the United States. Although some company names are immediately recognized as foreign owned, most give no outward indication of their ownership.

A company with foreign ownership presents several problems to a researcher. Because only a few foreign-owned corporations sell their shares in U.S. stock markets, the majority are not subject to U.S. financial reporting regulations. The familiar financial documents required of U.S. public corporations, which are standard sources of corporate information in this country, are not available for most foreign-owned firms. The foreign corporation with U.S. operations may report financial data to its own government and to stockholders abroad, but detailed, current information may be difficult to locate in this country. Also, the reporting requirements vary considerably in other nations. Foreign corporate documents may provide little, if any, insight into a firm's American operations and may not be printed in English.

Although many foreign-owned businesses in the United States operate under American-born or American-trained managers, the corporate attitude of a foreign firm toward information access may be more restrictive than that of its American-owned counterparts. The company may seek to avoid publicity for a variety of reasons and this may also hinder your search for information.

Small Local and Regional Companies

If a company is not publicly owned, foreign-owned, a subsidiary or division, or a large, privately held corporation, it is likely to be a small company with only local or regional interests. According to one source, of the estimated 20 million business firms in the United States in 1990, about 4.3 million or 21 percent were corporations (*The State of Small Business, 1990,* U.S. Government Printing Office, p. xii). Of those, approximately 16,000 are publicly owned. Perhaps another 200,000 are subsidiaries, foreign-owned, or major private corporations. The vast majority of remaining corporations fall into the category of small local or regional firms. In addition, nearly all are privately held.

Little information about small firms will be found in a library. If a company markets and sells its product only locally, few national publications will find it worthy of notice. Even a large company will be overlooked by reporters, analysts, investors, and publishers unless it is doing something unusual that captures outside attention. Don't mistake a lack of national prominence for a lack of success or good prospects. Small businesses are thriving. They provide excellent opportunities to gain experience. It will, however, take more than a hour or two to research one of them as a prospective employer.

IDENTIFYING PUBLIC OWNERSHIP

To determine quickly if a company is publicly owned, find out if it sells its shares of stock to the public on one of the U.S. stock exchanges or over-the-counter markets. The New York Stock Exchange (NYSE) and the American Stock Exchange (Amex or ASE), located on Wall Street in New York City, are the two largest and best known stock exchanges in the United States. They handle the stocks of the largest public corporations. The over-the-counter (OTC) markets handle the stock transactions of smaller public corporations. You may also see over-the-counter markets referred to as NASDAQ markets, an acronym derived from the information network of the OTC brokers' professional association, the National Association of Securities Dealers.

Start by checking the business section of a large newspaper. Both *The Wall Street Journal* and the *New York Times,* for example, print a daily list of stock market price quotations for companies traded on the NYSE, Amex, and OTC markets. All the companies whose stocks are listed are publicly owned corporations. (Newspapers in some smaller communities may abbreviate their stock listings, printing only those of high investor interest.) Another source of extensive stock quotation listings is the weekly financial news magazine, *Barron's.*

Newspaper stock quotation listings use 3- or 4-letter abbreviations of company names, which are usually easy to identify. Each stock exchange, however, is listed separately. If you are unsure which exchange a company might be listed on, check all three—the NYSE, Amex, and OTC listings.

Because companies that sell their stock in this way must file financial disclosure documents with the SEC, another quick method of determining whether a company is publicly owned is to see if it is in this directory:

Directory of Companies Required to File Annual Reports with the Securities and Exchange Commission. U.S. Securities and Exchange Commission. Annual.

> Listed here are more than 16,000 publicly owned companies that file financial disclosure reports with the SEC. Since the directory is a U.S. government publication, it will be available in many libraries. Notice in the example that the only information included in the directory is a company's name, its industry category, and the month its fiscal year ends (see Figure 3.1).

If you find that a company is listed as submitting reports to the SEC or as trading shares of stock, you have confirmed that it is a publicly owned corporation. You are ready to begin your research. Read Chapter 4 and investigate the suggestions there for finding information about public companies. Remember: *Publicly owned corporations will be easier to find information about than privately owned ones.*

INDUSTRY CODE MFG.	NON-MFG.	NAME	DOCKET NO.	FISCAL YEAR
2800		HOECHST CELANESE CORP	33-13326	12
3317		HOFMANN INDUSTRIES INC	2-70797	04
	7372	HOGAN SYSTEMS INC	0-12317	03
3580		HOH WATER TECHNOLOGY CORP	0-16416	10
	6799	HOLCO MORTGAGE ACCEPTANCE CORP I	1- 9485	12
	6189	HOLCO SECURED MORTGAGE INVESTMENT III	0-15335	12
2731		HOLDEN DAY INC	0- 5439	11
	6500	HOLDEN REAL ESTATE INCOME & GROWTH FUND	0-17608	12
	6552	HOLIDAY GULF HOMES INC	0- 7205	12
	7011	HOLIDAY INNS INC	1- 4804	01
3716		HOLIDAY RAMBLER CORP	33-12743	12
	5500	HOLIDAY RV SUPERSTORES INC	0-16448	10

Figure 3.1 Typical entries, reprinted from the *Directory of Companies Required to File Annual Reports with the Securities and Exchange Commission*, 1990 edition, published by the U.S. Securities and Exchange Commission.

IDENTIFYING SUBSIDIARY OR DIVISION STATUS

If a company is a part of a publicly owned corporation or a large private firm, it should not be difficult to confirm its status and learn its parent corporation's name. Begin by looking at one of these directories:

Directory of Corporate Affiliations. National Register Publishing Co. Annual.

> This guide to the corporate links of more than 4,000 major U.S. public and private companies includes public companies traded on the New York, American, and OTC exchanges as well as Fortune 1,000 and large private companies. As many as 40,000 divisions, subsidiaries, and affiliates are listed, many of them smaller companies not found in other directories.

America's Corporate Families (2 vols.). Dun & Bradstreet Information Services. Annual.

Listings cover 11,000 U.S. parent companies and their 67,000 plus subsidiaries, divisions, and major branches in the United States—a greater number than in the preceding directory. Each will have some unique listings despite considerable overlap.

Who Owns Whom. Dun & Bradstreet International. Annual.

Published in four regional world editions, the North American edition covers U.S., Canadian, and foreign parent corporations that have U.S. or Canadian subsidiaries. Subsidiary and associate companies and their place in the parent corporate structure are shown for each corporation, together with headquarters countries (see Figure 3.2).

If you cannot find any of these specialized directories, try this general business directory:

Standard & Poor's Register of Corporations, Directors, and Executives. Standard & Poor's Corp. Annual.

This directory has an "Ultimate Parent Index" that shows corporate affiliations for the 45,000 companies that it profiles.

PACIFIC GAS AND ELECTRIC CO., *77 Beale Street, San Francisco, Ca. 94106 Tel: (415)972-7000*	4931, 4923
Alberta Natural Gas Co. Ltd. (A)	Canada
Alberta and Southern Gas Co. Ltd.	Canada
Calaska Energy Co.	
Eureka Energy Co.	
Mission Trail Insurance (Cayman) Ltd.	Cayman Islands
Natural Gas Corp. of California	
NGC Production Co.	
PG & E Enterprises	
ANGUS Petroleum Corp.	
PG & E Generating Co.	
PG & E Operating Services Co.	
PG & E Properties Inc.	
PG & E Resources Co.	
Pacific Energy Services Co.	
Pacific California Gas System Inc.	
Pacific Conservation Services Co.	
Pacific Energy Fuels Co.	
Pacific Gas Properties Co.	
Pacific Gas Transmission Co.	
ANGUS Chemical Co. (A)	
ANGUS Chemie GmbH (A)	Germany
ANGUS Fine Chemicals Ltd. (A)	Republic of Ireland
Pacific Northwest Gas System Inc.	
Rocky Mountain Gas Transmission Co.	
Standard Pacific Gas Line Inc.	

Figure 3.2 Sample entry, reproduced from *Who Owns Whom: North America*, 1992, with permission from Dun & Bradstreet Ltd.

After you find a company listed as a subsidiary or division of another corporation in one of these directories, go to Chapter 5 for information suggestions based on this ownership type. You may also want to review the chapter on public or private corporations, depending on your company's parent organization, for additional ideas. Remember: *Subsidiaries or divisions will be more difficult to find information about than their parent corporations.*

IDENTIFYING FOREIGN OWNERSHIP

Foreign-owned companies are not usually difficult to identify, particularly if their name gives a clue to their origin. But you may be surprised to find that some companies with familiar names are foreign owned or controlled. Start a search to confirm a company's foreign ownership by checking one of these:

International Directory of Corporate Affiliations. National Register Publishing. Annual.

America's Corporate Families and International Affiliates. Dun & Bradstreet Information Services. Annual.

> Both of these directories list American subsidiaries of foreign parent corporations. The first focuses on foreign firms with affiliates in the United States and U.S. firms with foreign subsidiaries. The second covers more than 12,000 U.S. subsidiaries and their parent companies outside the United States as well as 1,500 U.S. parents with their subsidiaries.

Jeffrey S. Arpan and David A. Ricks. *Directory of Foreign Manufacturers in the United States,* 4th ed. Georgia State University Business Press. 1990.

> If a company is a manufacturer, this is a good place to begin. The directory has names and addresses of nearly 6,000 foreign-owned companies engaged in manufacturing, mining, and petroleum enterprises in the United States. The foreign parent corporation's name and country of origin are given for each company.

Directory of Foreign Investment in the U.S. Gale Research Inc. 1991.

> This volume briefly profiles foreign real estate and business investment in the United States. The business section includes 10,000 companies in all business lines that have 10 percent or more foreign ownership. As the example shows, brief directory information is provided for each U.S. firm and its foreign owner (see Figure 3.3).

The North American edition of *Who Owns Whom* was mentioned in the preceding section on subsidiaries. If a company was listed there as a subsidiary, was its parent a U.S. or foreign corporation?

After identifying a company as foreign-owned, go on to Chapter 6 and the suggestions outlined there for information. Be prepared for problems and disappointments as you begin,

★6768★
Novar Electronics Corporation
24 Brown St.
Barberton, OH 44203
216/745-0074
J. H. Ott

Description: Acquired in late 1989 for $27.8 million. *Annual Sales:* $11,100.000. *Employees:* 132. **Owner:** R.T.Z. Corporation PLC. *Address:* 6 St. James Square, London, GL SW1Y 4LD, England. *SIC:* 3669.

★6769★
Oki America, Inc.
1 University Plaza
Hackensack, NJ 07601
201/646-0011
H. Atagi

Description: *Employees:* 15. **Owner:** Oki Electric Industrial Company Ltd. *Address:* 1-7-12 Toranomon, Minatoku, Tokyo 105. Japan. *SIC:* 3661.

Figure 3.3 Typical entries, *Directory of Foreign Investment in the U.S.*, First edition, edited by Nancy Garman. Copyright © 1991 by Gale Research Inc. Reproduced by permission of the publisher.

however, as fewer research options will be available for foreign firms. Remember: *Foreign-owned companies may be more difficult to find information about than American-owned companies.*

IDENTIFYING PRIVATE OWNERSHIP

One quick way to learn if a company is privately owned, particularly if it is a large company with a national market, is to check this directory:

Directory of Leading Private Companies. National Register Publishing Co. Annual.

> Only the largest private companies, with sales exceeding $10 million, are included in this directory—a total of about 7,000 companies. The wholly owned subsidiaries of these firms are also listed, as the example shows (see Figure 3.4).

If you have access to a limited library collection which does not include directories of private companies, ask a librarian to recommend general business directories for you to check. Most include both private and public companies and indicate the ownership type of a company. Here's one example:

Ward's Business Directory of U.S. Private and Public Companies. Gale Research Inc. Annual.

> Over 100,000 businesses are listed, both public and private. Beginning in 1991, there is no minimum size criteria for inclusion. Each listing indicates the company type—public, private, division, subsidiary, joint venture, or affiliate.

Once you are certain that a company is privately held, you are ready for the information sources suggested for private companies in Chapter 7. You will encounter a number of barriers as you proceed in your research, many more than for a publicly held company. Public companies, however, have no monopoly in providing great jobs, excellent workplaces, and

• 38553-000

HARBOUR GROUP LTD.
7701 Forsyth Blvd.
Clayton, MO 63105
Tel.: 314-727-5550 **DE**
Telefax: 314-727-0941
Telefax: 314-727-9912
Year Founded: 1976
Sales: $240,000,000
Emp: 3,000
Holding Co.: Mfr. of Expendable Cutting Tools, Medical Equip., Indus. & Submersible Pumps, Optical Prods., Master Alloys
S.I.C.: 6719; 3545; 3561; 3841; 3842; 3827; 3325; 3423
Sam Fox (*Chm. Bd. & Chief Exec. Officer*)
Ralph Lobdell (*Pres.*)
James C. Janning (*Chief Oper. Officer*)
Samuel Hamacher (*Chief Fin. Officer*)
Brenda Slimmer (*Dir.-Data Processing*)
No. of Mfg. Plants/Facilities: 14
No. of U.S. Offices: 1

Outside Service Firms:

22261-054
Price Waterhouse (*Accounting Firm*)
St. Louis, MO

31151-001
Bank of Boston (*Commercial Banker*)
Atlanta, GA

4454-000
Dickstein, Shapiro & Morin (*Legal Firm*)
Washington, DC

Wholly-Owned Subsidiaries:

38553-002
Burks Pumps Inc.
1434 No. 22nd St.
Decatur, IL 62526
Tel.: 217-429-2591
Mfr. of Centrifugal, Turbine & Submersible Pumps, Condensate Return & Boiler Feed Systems
S.I.C.: 3561
C.J. Sears (*Pres.*)

38553-001
Carbide International Inc.
299 Bond
Elk Grove Village, IL 60007
Tel.: 312-593-5500
Rick Stretcher (*Pres.*)
Thomas Pratt (*V.P.-Fin.*)

Figure 3.4 Typical entry, *Directory of Leading Private Companies,* 1989 edition. Published by National Register Publishing Co., a division of Reed Reference Publishing Company. Used by permission.

first-class opportunities. Spend time and ingenuity in researching a private company—it may pay off with the perfect job for you. Remember: *Privately held corporations will be more difficult to find information about than publicly owned ones.*

IDENTIFYING A SMALL LOCAL OR REGIONAL COMPANY

Unlike the other categories of ownership types, no directory devoted exclusively to small companies of primarily local interest is available. National business directories include a few small companies with high annual sales or net worth. Some communities publish their own business directories, but these are seldom available outside that community, except by special request. Because some corporate structures are complex, an affiliate or division of a larger company can occasionally be overlooked, making identification difficult. Also, many companies shun publicity and prefer not to be identified. If you are unable to verify that a company belongs in any of the other categories, you are most likely to decide by default that it belongs in this group.

You may have to spend extra time and use your ingenuity to track down facts on a small company, for published materials will not be a primary information source. Still, don't give up on these smaller firms; a number of information possibilities do exist, and Chapter 8 details how to research them. Scan the suggestions for large private companies in Chapter 7 for additional ideas. Most important of all, don't write off a small company as lacking the potential to be a great employer. First do your homework on the firm and then decide if you should give it serious consideration. Remember: *Small local or regional firms will be more difficult to find information about than large, nationally known corporations.*

PART II

RESEARCHING A PROSPECTIVE EMPLOYER

4 Researching Publicly Owned U.S. Corporations

If you are researching a company that trades its shares of stock on a U.S. stock exchange and files financial disclosure statements with the U.S. Securities and Exchange Commission (SEC), many published sources can provide information. In financial terms, the company is one of several thousand large corporations that are often well known to the general public. A library will have most, if not all, of the information you need to evaluate it as a prospective employer (see Figure 4.1).

DIRECTORIES

Begin your research by looking at one of the most widely available sources of information—a directory. Hundreds of business directories are published each year. They are logical starting points for many kinds of research, but particularly for information about individual companies. Simply by consulting a directory, you can find several of the factors you should consider when evaluating a company.

Directories provide the backbone of company information: addresses and telephone numbers. Many include the names of

Look for ***Location*** in

- Directories
- Annual Reports
- 10-K Reports

Look for ***Facilities*** in

- Directories
- Annual Reports
- 10-K Reports
- Credit Reports
- Articles
- Personal Contacts

Look for ***Company Size*** in

- Directories
- Annual Reports
- 10-K Reports
- Credit Reports
- Articles
- Business Rankings

Look for ***Product/Service*** in

- Directories
- Annual Reports
- 10-K Reports
- Financial Services
- Credit Reports
- Articles
- Industry Surveys

Look for ***Financial Data*** in

- Annual Reports
- 10-K Reports
- Financial Services
- Credit Reports
- Advisory Services
- Brokerage Reports
- Articles
- Industry Averages

Look for ***Company History*** in

- Annual Reports
- 10-K Reports
- Financial Services
- Articles
- Published Histories

Look for ***Company Strategies*** in

- Annual Reports
- 10-K Reports
- Advisory Services
- Brokerage Reports
- Articles
- Personal Contacts

Look for ***Response to Difficulty*** in

- Annual Reports
- 10-K Reports
- Articles
- Personal Contacts

Look for ***Management/Employee Data*** in

- Annual Reports
- 10-K Reports
- Articles
- Personal Contacts

Look for ***Executive Biography*** in

- Directories
- Annual Reports
- 10-K Reports
- Articles
- Personal Contacts

Look for ***Employee Morale*** in

- Articles
- Personal Contacts

Look for ***Salaries*** in

- Books
- Periodicals/Newspapers
- Employment Offices
- Personal Contacts

Look for ***Industry Outlook*** in

- Investment Services
- Brokerage Reports
- Articles
- Industry Surveys
- Trade Associations
- Personal Contacts

Figure 4.1 Research checklist for a publicly owned company.

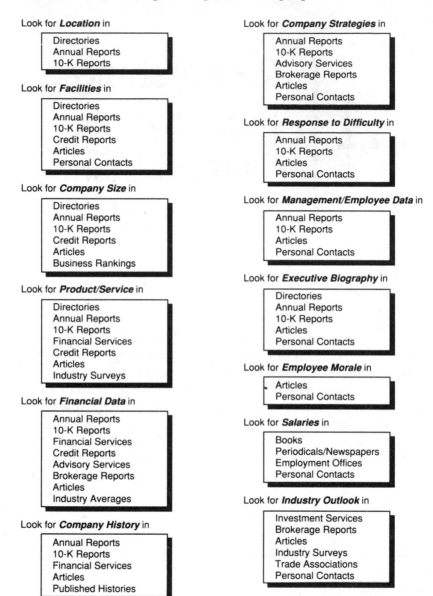

top executives, product lines, number of employees, and approximate annual sales. Depending on the purpose and scale of the directory, some identify the purchasing manager, the personnel officer, or other executives. Others may note a company's export-import participation, industry rank, advertising expenditure, or additional features.

National Business Directories

No single business directory lists every company in the United States. National business directories, however, will list the largest and most significant companies. Any one of the best known and most widely available national business directories will provide basic facts about a publicly owned corporation. Each may also contain unique facts. Check all of them, if available. They include:

Million Dollar Directory. Dun & Bradstreet Information Services. Annual.

> This may be the most widely known U.S. business directory. It covers 160,000 businesses, both publicly and privately owned. The criteria for being included are sales volume of over $25 million, 250 or more employees, or net worth of at least $750,000. Each company headquarters location is listed, together with its SIC number and product lines, D-U-N-S (R) number, annual sales, number of employees, chief officers, ticker symbol banking and accounting relationships, and state of incorporation. Where applicable, stock exchange or parent company is noted. One index volume lists companies by Standard Industrial Classification (SIC) numbers, or product lines, indicating other companies in the industry. (SIC codes, which were developed by the U.S. government to organize and interpret economic and industry data, are based on a numeric system and are commonly two to four digits, although more are possible. Many business publishers, as well as the federal government, use the codes to classify information by product or service.) A second index arranged geographically allows you to identify other companies located near the one you are researching. The *Million Dollar Directory* alone answers several initial questions about a company (see Figure 4.2).

	D-U-N-S 00-657-4790	**EXP**
▲ **BENTLEY & CO** (DE)		
100 NW Main St, Washburg, IL		
Zip 61629	*Tel* (309) 555-2100	
Sales 11100MM	*Emp* 59900 *YS** 1925	
Tkr Sym BTL	*Exch* BSE CIN MSE NYS PBS PCS	
SIC 7361 7363 Employment agencies; temporary help service.		
Bk Congressional Bk NA, Chicago, IL		
Accts Proven Way		
* Donald V Franks	Ch Bd CEO	
* John B Wogsland	Pr	
Len A Kuchan	Sec	
Thomas Tartaglia	Ex VP, Finance	
Anthony Tongo	Sr VP	
James Linch	VP, Sales	

Figure 4.2 Typical entry, *Million Dollar Directory*. Copyright 1992 Dun & Bradstreet Inc. All rights reserved. Reprinted with permission.

Standard & Poor's Register of Corporations, Directors, and Executives. Standard & Poor's Corp. Annual.

A highly respected and widely known directory, *S&P's Register* covers 45,000 corporations chosen on the basis of their interest of the business world. Volume One contains the listings by company name. Here you find the headquarters address, officers and directors, annual revenue, number of employees, stock exchange, and business lines for each company. An index volume provides listings by SIC numbers and by geographic location.

Thomas Register of American Manufacturers. Thomas Publishing Co. Annual.

Thomas Register is also well known and widely available. The set of over 20 volumes provides a comprehensive directory of nearly 150,000 American manufacturers and their products. Two volumes—the "Company Profiles"—are an alphabetical list of the manufacturers. Because the directory emphasizes the product rather than the company, the information in the "Company Profiles" is brief. Usually only headquarters address, telephone number, and product lines are listed, but additional manufacturing locations are often noted, as you will see in the example. Each company is assigned an "asset rating" that gives a general idea of the company's size according to tangible assets. Don't overlook the advertisements interspersed throughout the set and the company catalogs that fill the final volumes. They may provide clues to how a company markets its products (see Figure 4.3).

Ward's Business Directory of U.S. Private and Public Companies. Gale Research Inc. Annual.

This directory covers over 100,000 companies, both public and private. Beginning with the 1991 edition, there is no financial size restriction for inclusion. Although a few businesses with less than $500,000 in sales are included, most are far larger. Company data is similar to that of the preceding directories; *Ward's* also indicates the company founding date and type. One

Bruning Paint Co. (Architectural Paints, Stains, Enamels, Masonry Waterproofing Systems, Metal Primers, Clear Wood Finishes, Traffic Marking Paint & Catalyzed Epoxies), 601-T S. Haven St., Baltimore, MD 21224 (Br. At Pompano Beach, FL) (Ex.) (NR)............301—342-3636

Bruning & Federle Mfg. Co. (Bruning & Federle Mfrg. Co.) (S—Bruning & Federle Mfg. Co) (Dust Collection, Pneumatic Conveying & Ventilating Systems, Material Handling Blowers, Rotary Airlocks), 2503-T Northside Dr., Statesville, NC 28677 (Br. at Stateville, NC; Emporia, Virginia) (1M–) (FAX: 704-878-0647).................... 704—873-7237

BRUNK

BRUNK INDUSTRIES, INC., 1225 Sage St. At Hwy. 36, P.O. Drawer 310, Lake Geneva, WI 53147 (1M+) (TELEX: 888-6665; FAX: 414-248-2726, Dept. 100).................................... 414—248-8873
(Custom Precision Stampings For The Electronics, Computer, Office Products, Automotive, Marine, Medical Industries & Military, Including Laminations For Motor & Electrical Applications. In-House Capabilities To Design & Build AAA Tooling. Wire EDM. High Speed, Large Volume & Long Run Capabilities. Assemblies, Sub-Assemblies & Secondary Operations Including Tapping, Deburring, Heat Treating, Plating, Welding, Riveting, Painting. Mfr. Of Reed Valves & Assemblies. Mfr. Of Bandolier Pins For The Electronics & Computer Industry)
(Ex.) (P. & Chf. Eng.) B. Brunk; (Exec. V.P.) L. Brunk; (S., T.) U. Brunk; (V.P. & Plt. Mgr.) K. Andersson

▲ SEE OUR CATALOG IN CATALOG FILE SECTION

Figure 4.3 Typical entries, *Thomas Register of American Manufacturers,* 1991 edition. Reprinted by permission of Thomas Publishing Company.

volume of *Ward's* ranks companies by sales within industry categories, giving an idea of a firm's chief competitors and their comparative share of the market.

All these directories may be available in some libraries in electronic format as compact disc products or as online databases. See Chapter 12 for more about electronic information sources.

Specialized Business Directories

In addition to the widely known, comprehensive national business directories, there are many kinds of specialized directories. Some list only manufacturers in a single industry; others categorize companies by product line, such as all textile suppliers, manufacturers, wholesalers, and retailers. An example of such a specialized directory is:

Dun's Industrial Guide: The Metalworking Directory. Dun & Bradstreet Information Services. Annual.

This is a comprehensive guide to 80,000 manufacturing plants, distributors, and firms, providing standard directory information for each organization. For manufacturers, the following are also listed: end products manufactured, principal manufacturing processes performed, principal metal products purchased, and the form purchased in. For distributors, the listings include the metal distributed and its form, the processes performed, and warehouse space available. Since only firms employing 20 or more are included, the directory provides a thorough list of industrial production companies.

Other specialized directories add a further dimension to knowledge of a corporation in a particular area. Examples include:

National Directory of Corporate Public Affairs. Columbia Books, Inc. Annual.

To track a corporation's role in government and community affairs, try this directory of some 1,600 companies, both publicly and privately owned. Each company listing includes the address, telephone number, and key public affairs personnel of its headquarters office, its Washington, DC, office, its political action committee (PAC) office, and its corporate foundation office. Of special interest are the major PAC contributions and foundation fund recipients noted for each corporation (see Figure 4.4).

Directory of American Research and Technology. R. R. Bowker. Annual.

If you are seeking information on a company's research and development activity, this directory may help. It lists over 11,000 laboratories and R&D centers that report to corporations and other nongovernment organizations. Included for each unit listed are the number of staff with advanced degrees and areas of research activity within the unit.

Ad $ Summary. Leading National Advertisers. Quarterly.

For an indication of a corporation's spending on advertising for consumer products, try this directory. Total corporate media spending for a specific product brand is noted and a ranking of top corporate advertisers is included.

If you are curious about specialized directories available for a specific type of company or a special factor you are interested in, ask your reference librarian for this guide:

Directories in Print. Gale Research Inc. Annual.

Here are listed and described over 14,000 directories of all kinds, including many business and trade directories. A keyword index helps to determine what is available for an industry or subject. If you identify a directory you would like to scan for information, check its availability in your library. Should you want to purchase a copy of a directory listed, each entry notes the publisher and price.

If *Directories in Print* or an alternative guide to directories is not available, simply check your library's catalog to see what special directories might be in its collection.

Beech Aircraft Corp.

A builder of aircraft for commercial and defense/aerospace markets and maker of missile targets. A subsidiary of Raytheon Co.

P.O. Box 85, Wichita, KS 67201-0085 Tel. (316) 676-7111

Washington Office:

1215 Jefferson Davis Hwy., 15th Floor, Arlington, VA 22202-4302
Tel. (703) 521-2020

Contact: Bill Butler, Director, Government Relations

Political Action Committee:

Beech Aircraft PAC (BeechPAC) • P.O. Box 85, Wichita, KS 67201-0085
Tel. (316) 676-7145

Contributed to Candidates: $29,300 (1/89–7/90)

Gave to 24 Democrats ($18,950) and 13 Republicans ($10,350) Principal recipients: Senate—Gave $1,000 to each of 8 candidates. House—Bob Carr (D-MI), $1,700; Daniel Glickman (D-KS), $1,350.

Corporate Foundation / Contributions:

Beech Aircraft Foundation • P.O. Box 85, Wichita, KS 67201-0085
Tel. (316) 676-8177

Annual Grant Total: $400,000–$500,000

Assets: $5,525,000 (1988)

Preference: giving centered on the Wichita, KS region, with some donations to national groups. Primary interests: higher education, community and civic groups, youth groups, united funds. Past recipients: United Fund of Wichita, Colonial Williamsburg Foundation.

Publications:

BacTalk • Quarterly. • Circulation: 8,700.
Beechcraft Marketing Report • Quarterly. • Circulation: 3,500.
Beechcrafter • Bi-monthly. • Circulation: 10,100.

Public Affairs and Related Activities Personnel:

At Main Office:

GREGORY, James M., Director, Corporate Affairs
(316) 676-7689
Serves also as Vice Chairman and Treasurer, Beech Aircraft PAC.
Registered as lobbyist in Kansas.

LAWRENCE, Larry E., Secretary and Treasurer, Beech Aircraft Foundation
(316) 676-7111

POTTS, Michael S., Manager, Public Relations
(316) 676-8674

ZERBE, Pat, Manager, Corporate Communications
(316) 676-7602
Serves also as Editor of BacTalk and Beechcraft Marketing Report.

At Washington, DC Office:

BUTLER, Bill, Director, Government Relations
(703) 521-2020

Figure 4.4 Typical entry, *National Directory of Corporate Public Affairs,* 1991 edition. Reprinted by permission of Columbia Books, Inc.

State Directories

An additional option to investigate is a state industrial directory. Each of the 50 states has a directory covering the manufacturers within its borders. An advantage of these directories is that they profile individual plant locations within a state, rather than the corporate headquarters usually found in national directories. Because of this, you can find unique information here. Local managers, plant size, number of employees, and products manufactured are commonly included for each manufacturing location listed. The state directories are usually restricted to manufacturers, but some larger states also have directories of nonmanufacturing firms. Most libraries will have the directory for their state; some may have those of all states.

Use directories for information about:

- Location
- Facilities
- Company Size
- Product/Service
- Executive Biography

FINANCIAL REPORTS AND STATEMENTS

Financial data provides a core of vital information for publicly owned companies. If you are researching such a company, its SEC financial disclosure reports and the annual report to stockholders should be at the top of your "must read" list. You may be familiar with annual reports, but the 10-K report that publicly owned companies file each year with the SEC is less well known.

Annual Reports

Annual reports are the glossy brochures mailed each year to a corporation's stockholders to summarize the year's performance and accomplishments. In addition to annual financial statements, they usually contain interesting graphics, a smiling portrait of the board of directors, and an upbeat narrative report. The annual report is sometimes regarded as a public relations effort as much as a financial report. It is true that it usually presents a company's condition in the best possible way. The financial statements are independently audited for accuracy, however, and all narrative discussion must be consistent with the financial statements. Some reports do acknowledge business downturns. Nevertheless, bad news is usually minimized or glossed over where possible.

Despite these drawbacks, annual reports contain much potentially useful information. A good report has several sections you will want to study carefully. Start by looking at the "Letter to the Stockholders" written by the president or chairman of the board. These reviews of a company's current situation and its outlook for the future vary in content and length, but most give a good sense of the company's mood. Look carefully here for insights into the company's management goals and its strategic plans. After the president's letter, read the "Auditor's Report," which is a signed statement by the independent accounting firm verifying the accuracy of the financial report. Note especially any reservations or qualifying remarks that might appear here. Finally, look over the financial statements, including the footnotes, for the company's financial standing. The footnotes are important for explaining any unusual circumstances not obvious from the figures alone. Many companies include a 5 to 10 year summary of financial highlights.

Although the financial statements may provide the key data in the annual report, don't neglect the management narrative. If you want to pick up supplementary facts about a company, this is often a good source for items such as business strategies, operating objectives, R&D prospects, corporate strengths, marketing highlights, expansion plans, international operations, and government contracts. In other words, almost anything that will help the stockholder interpret the company's present performance and see its future direction may be discussed. This information can also aid in evaluating the company as an employer. A copy of any publicly owned company's annual report may be requested directly from the corporate office at little or no cost. Annual report collections are also found in many libraries.

10-K Reports

The 10-K report is a detailed financial disclosure report, submitted annually to the U.S. Securities and Exchange Commission by publicly owned corporations. Unlike the annual report, 10-K reports contain no glossy photos and no hype. They are unembellished documents with data set out in clearly defined categories as required by the SEC. Although the content of the 10-K and the annual report are becoming increasingly comparable for many companies, there are differences. Look closely at what is included in the 10-K.

Part I of the 10-K asks for the following information:

1. *Business.* This covers products and services, markets, and distribution methods. It may also include, if significant, competitive factors; backlog; raw material availability; the importance of patents, licenses, or franchises; cost of research; total number of employees; and compliance with environmental laws. Each line of business or product category, sometimes referred to as a business segment, must be separately discussed.
2. *Properties.* The location of all plants and properties owned or leased is given.
3. *Legal Proceedings.* Any litigation currently pending is summarized.
4. *Shareholders' Voting.* When did shareholders meet and what items were on the ballot?

Part II of the 10-K contains the financial data. This includes discussion of the company's stocks—prices and dividends paid, five years of selected financial data, and a management discussion of the financial condition. In the management discussion, the firm must specifically comment on any significant financial data and explain why it is important.

Part III of the 10-K concerns the company's management and supplies background data for all directors and executive officers. Remuneration and stock holdings for top officers are noted. Owners of 5 percent or more of the company's stock are also identified.

10-K reports are less readily available than annual reports. Generally they are not sent to stockholders, but they may be requested from the SEC or from a private document service for a fee. The SEC accepts only written requests and service is somewhat slow, taking as long as two or three weeks. (For information on requesting documents from the SEC, write or call the Public Reference Room, U.S. Securities and Exchange Commission, 450 Fifth Street NW, Washington, DC 20549, 202-272-7450.) An alternative is provided by the private document delivery service, Disclosure, Inc., of Bethesda, Maryland (Disclosure, Inc., 5161 River Road, Bethesda MD 20816, 800-638-8241). Either paper or microfiche copies of the 10-K reports can be speedily delivered by Disclosure at a cost of approximately $20 to $35 per report. Many larger libraries carry 10-K reports, often in microfiche format. *Compact D/SEC,* a compact disc product containing data extracted from the 10-K and other documents, is also available in many large libraries.

Comprehensive Financial Services

If you do not have access to annual reports or SEC documents or if you want only a quick review of a company's financial status, use one of the published financial services. These services rely on the primary financial documents, the annual reports and the 10-K, for data. They summarize the pertinent material and reorganize it into an easy-to-use format, revised and updated on a regular basis. The two best-known services, available in many libraries, are:

Moody's Manuals. Moody's Investors Service. Annual with updates.

> The Manuals are a series of eight titles that report on nearly 25,000 firms in a variety of business areas. Included are companies listed on U.S. stock exchanges and major financial institutions. The information for each company usually includes a brief corporate history, with the founding date, mergers, and name changes. Next, business lines and products, plants and properties, and any subsidiaries are listed. A summary financial

statement with three to seven years of data follows. The data is in an abbreviated form and will not include the footnotes found in the annual report. A third section outlines the current status of a company's stocks and bonds. Moody's assigns a rating to the bonds to indicate investment safety. Titles in the series include: *Bank and Finance Manual, Industrial Manual, International Manual, Municipal and Government Manual, OTC Industrial Manual, OTC Unlisted Manual, Public Utility Manual,* and *Transportation Manual.* To locate a company's report, use the separately published index. Weekly or semiweekly updates accompany each manual.

Standard & Poor's Corporation Records. Standard & Poor's Corp. Annual with updates.

Similar in content and scope to *Moody's Manuals,* this set is arranged in alphabetical sequence. It covers perhaps a third fewer companies than Moody's, omitting municipalities and banks and covering financial institutions minimally. It has both a narrative and a financial profile of each company, including two or more years of comparative data. Like *Moody's,* this service rates bonds for investment security. The *Corporation Records* are updated daily with news of corporate earnings, mergers, new security offerings, bond rate changes, business failures, and so on.

Both of these sources may be available in electronic format in some libraries.

Business Credit Reports

Credit rating reports are prepared for the use of organizations that extend credit or lend money to business clients. They contain financial data and sometimes additional information about a company. They are based on information supplied by banks, creditors, public records, and the company itself. The reports are considered confidential and are sold only to financial organizations and to businesses and individuals with legitimate need for them. They are not available to a company's business competitors or to the general public. As a result, you will not find them in libraries. However, excerpts from the reports are available as online databases in many libraries. Unfortunately, these are expensive databases to search: The cost of obtaining a single credit report may range from $25 to $100 or more, should one be available. Unless you have difficulty gaining information in other ways, this option for access to financial data for publicly owned companies should probably be only a last resort.

After reading the annual report, the 10-K report, and a profile in either *Moody's Manuals* or *Standard & Poor's Corporation Records,* you may have answers to most of your questions about a publicly owned company. You may be tempted to stop at this point. However, if you want to research a company thoroughly, consider the additional suggestions in this chapter.

Use financial reports and statements for information about:

- Location
- Facilities
- Company Size
- Product/Service
- Financial Data
- Company History
- Company Strategies
- Response to Difficulty
- Management/Employee Data
- Executive Biography

INVESTMENT ADVISORY PUBLICATIONS

When considering a company's financial standing, it is also useful to look at its rating as an investment prospect. Although employment, not investment, is your goal, factors that influence an investment rating may also affect a company's potential as a good employer. These include, for example, the company's financial health, its outlook for growth, its new products and expansion plans, and its competitive status.

Advisory Services

Publications that provide this analysis are known as investment advisory services. They vary from well-known, established publications with wide readership to newsletters of brief duration and limited audience. The advisory services with wide readership will be most valuable to you. Read others with caution, for they may be less balanced in their advice or recommend action based on a particular investment theory. Don't forget you are interested in a company as an employer, not an investment prospect, and base your conclusions about the company on that fact. The following are reliable and widely available investment services:

Value Line Investment Survey. Value Line, Inc. Weekly.

> This well-known service includes reports and analysis on a rotating quarterly basis for approximately 2,000 publicly owned corporations in over 90 industries. Each company report is a one-page summary. Included are a 10 to 15 year statistical history of key investment factors plus estimates of the company's stock performance over the next 3 to 5 years. For investors, a key *Value Line* feature is its rating of each stock for timeliness and safety. For you, the most important feature may be the narrative paragraphs, which analyze a company's current position and its future prospects. However, don't overlook the many other details of a company's financial status and outlook that can be found here (see Figure 4.5).

Standard Stock Reports. Standard & Poor's Corp. Quarterly.

> Brief two-page reports for companies listed on the New York, American, and over-the-counter stock exchanges make it easy to determine at a quick glance what a company does, any recent corporate developments, and its current outlook. Ten years of summary financial data give a view of trends. A letter ranking indicates S&P's preferences for investment based on growth and stability of earnings and on dividends paid.

Moody's Handbook of Common Stocks. Moody's Investors Service. Quarterly.

> This volume contains concise one-page profiles with financial statistics for the stocks of 1,000 companies of high investor interest. Moody's grades each stock—high, investment, medium, or speculative—and adds a short statement of company characteristics.

CIRCUIT CITY STORES NYSE-CC

RECENT PRICE	P/E RATIO	RELATIVE P/E RATIO	DIV'D YLD	VALUE LINE
22	15.2 (Trailing: 18.8 Median: 12.0)	1.03	0.5%	1674

TIMELINESS (Relative Price Performance Next 12 Mos.) 2 Above Average
SAFETY 3 Average
(Scale: 1 Highest to 5 Lowest)
BETA 1.40 (1.00 = Market)

1994-96 PROJECTIONS

	Price	Gain	Ann'l Total Return
High	60	(+175%)	*29%*
Low	40	(+80%)	*17%*

Insider Decisions

	J	F	M	A	M	J	J	A	S
to Buy	0	0	0	0	0	0	1	1	1
Options	0	1	0	0	0	2	2	0	0
to Sell	0	0	0	0	3	1	0	0	0

Institutional Decisions

	4Q'90	1Q'91	2Q'91
to Buy	58	70	60
to Sell	60	56	58
Hld's(000)	33527	35353	31091

	1980	1981	1982	1983	1984	1985	1986	1987	1988	1989	1990	1991
High:	0.4	0.8	1.0	4.5	7.4	7.8	17.1	20.8	22.6	27.0	29.0	26.0
Low:	0.3	0.3	0.4	0.9	2.9	4.7	5.9	8.5	9.3	17.7	9.0	11.3

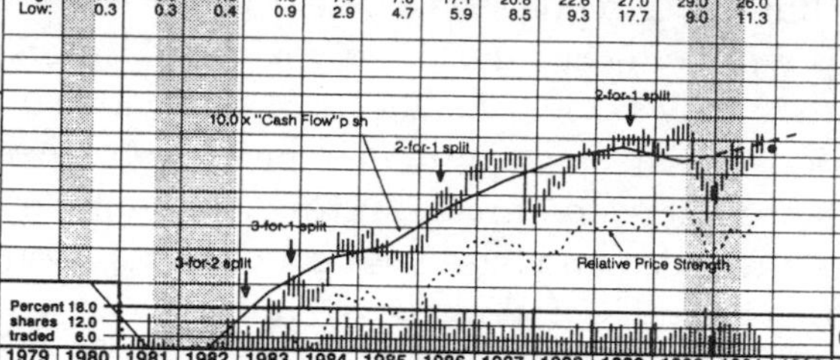

Target Price Range
1994 | 1995 | 1996

Shaded areas indicate recessions

Options: PACE

1975	1976	1977	1978	1979	1980	1981	1982	1983	1984	1985	1986	1987	1988	1989	1990	1991	1992	© VALUE LINE PUB., INC.	94-96
2.50	2.81	3.52	4.31	4.48	4.99	5.32	7.29	9.02	11.95	16.11	22.77	30.14	38.06	45.72	51.08	*59.25*	*67.95*	Sales per sh A	*113.25*
d.11	.11	.10	.12	.11	.14	.10	.18	.36	.54	.64	1.01	1.43	1.91	2.18	1.85	*2.20*	*2.70*	"Cash Flow"per sh	*5.00*
d.13	.04	.08	.09	.08	.10	.06	.12	.31	.49	.50	.80	1.13	1.53	1.70	1.22	*1.45*	*1.85*	Earnings per sh B	*3.50*
--	--	--	--	.01	.01	.01	.01	.01	.02	.02	.03	.04	.06	.08	.10	*.10*	*.12*	Div'ds Decl'd per sh C	*.25*
.16	.21	.32	.41	.49	.58	.59	.72	1.21	2.04	2.54	3.36	4.50	6.05	7.83	7.92	*9.35*	*11.40*	Book Value per sh D	*21.25*
24.45	25.77	25.77	25.89	26.72	26.41	33.11	33.74	39.53	43.45	43.78	44.38	44.80	45.23	45.86	46.34	*47.00*	*47.75*	Common Shs Outst'g E	*50.30*
--	4.1	4.3	3.4	4.1	3.6	8.7	6.0	9.8	11.2	12.5	16.2	13.7	11.4	13.4	15.8	*Bold figures are*		Avg Ann'l P/E Ratio	*14.0*
--	.52	.56	.46	.59	.48	1.06	.66	.83	1.04	1.01	1.10	.92	.95	1.01	1.17	*Value Line*		Relative P/E Ratio	*1.15*
--	--	--	.4%	1.6%	1.6%	1.3%	1.4%	.3%	.3%	.4%	.2%	.3%	.3%	.4%	.5%	*estimates*		Avg Ann'l Div'd Yield	*.5%*

CAPITAL STRUCTURE as of 8/31/91
Total Debt $95.0 mill. **Due in 5 Yrs** $72.9 mill.
LT Debt $92.9 mill. **LT Interest** $8.1 mill.
Incl. $33.0 mill. capitalized leases.
(LT interest earned: 11.5x; total interest coverage: 7.9x) (19% of Cap'l)

Leases, Uncapitalized Annual rentals $42.3 mill.

Pension Liability None

Pfd Stock None

Common Stock 46,629,552 shs. as of 9/30/91 (81% of Cap'l)

1981	1982	1983	1984	1985	1986	1987	1988	1989	1990	1991	1992	© VALUE LINE PUB., INC.	94-96
176.2	245.9	356.7	519.2	705.5	1010.7	1350.4	1721.5	2096.6	2366.9	*2785*	*3245*	Sales ($mill) A	*5700*
27.0%	28.1%	28.8%	28.6%	28.3%	28.7%	28.8%	29.2%	29.5%	29.1%	*29.0%*	*29.0%*	Gross Margin	*29.5%*
97	101	98	93	69	87	105	119	145	171	*195*	*220*	Number of Stores F	*300*
1.9	4.3	12.0	20.2	22.0	35.3	50.4	69.5	78.1	56.7	*70.0*	*90.0*	Net Profit ($mill)	*185*
43.6%	46.2%	46.2%	46.8%	45.0%	50.6%	43.5%	39.3%	39.0%	38.0%	*37.5%*	*38.0%*	Income Tax Rate	*39.0%*
1.1%	1.8%	3.4%	3.9%	3.1%	3.5%	3.7%	4.0%	3.7%	2.4%	*2.5%*	*2.8%*	Net Profit Margin	*3.2%*
6.8	7.4	7.5	7.0	6.0	7.0	6.5	5.7	6.3	6.1	*6.4*	*6.5*	Inventory Turnover	*6.8*
16.7	23.1	45.7	71.1	56.6	97.3	149.2	174.7	220.0	189.4	*205*	*280*	Working Cap'l ($mill)	*720*
13.5	13.3	15.2	27.9	40.0	101.2	96.7	94.7	93.9	94.3	*90.0*	*90.0*	Long-Term Debt ($mill)	*80.0*
20.1	24.8	48.6	89.2	111.8	149.3	201.4	273.6	359.3	366.9	*440*	*545*	Net Worth ($mill)	*1065*
8.7%	12.7%	19.6%	17.9%	15.1%	15.0%	18.2%	19.9%	18.1%	13.2%	*14.0%*	*14.5%*	% Earned Total Cap'l	*16.5%*
9.6%	17.4%	24.7%	22.7%	19.7%	23.6%	25.0%	25.4%	21.7%	15.4%	*16.0%*	*16.5%*	% Earned Net Worth	*17.5%*
8.6%	16.1%	24.0%	21.9%	18.8%	22.8%	24.2%	24.5%	20.8%	14.3%	*14.5%*	*15.5%*	% Retained to Comm Eq	*16.0%*
13%	10%	4%	4%	5%	4%	3%	4%	4%	8%	*7%*	*6%*	% All Div'ds to Net Prof	*7%*

CURRENT POSITION ($MILL.)	1989	1990	8/31/91
Cash Assets	91.7	25.2	30.1
Receivables	9.8	26.7	43.2
Inventory (Avg Cost)	331.2	389.8	501.8
Other	9.5	8.7	13.6
Current Assets	442.2	450.4	588.7
Accts Payable	165.5	194.5	312.7
Debt Due	2.0	15.1	2.1
Other	54.7	51.4	33.0
Current Liab.	222.2	261.0	347.8

ANNUAL RATES of change (per sh)	Past 10 Yrs.	Past 5 Yrs.	Est'd '88-'90 to '94-'96
Sales	25.5%	29.5%	*16.5%*
"Cash Flow"	32.0%	31.0%	*16.5%*
Earnings	32.0%	28.0%	*15.5%*
Dividends	34.0%	36.5%	*21.5%*
Book Value	31.0%	30.5%	*19.5%*

Fiscal Year Begins	QUARTERLY SALES ($ mill.) A May 31	Aug.31	Nov.30	Feb.28	Full Fiscal Year
1988	327.6	396.1	434.3	563.5	1721.5
1989	408.0	471.6	525.9	691.1	2096.6
1990	490.1	550.6	585.0	741.2	2366.9
1991	562.2	634.8	*690*	*898*	*2785*
1992	*630*	*730*	*810*	*1075*	*3245*

Fiscal Year Begins	EARNINGS PER SHARE A B May 31	Aug.31	Nov.30	Feb.28	Full Fiscal Year
1988	.20	.37	.30	.66	1.53
1989	.23	.37	.32	.78	1.70
1990	.23	.36	.05	.58	1.22
1991	.17	.37	*.18*	*.73*	*1.45*
1992	*.26*	*.41*	*.27*	*.91*	*1.85*

Calendar	QUARTERLY DIVIDENDS PAID C Mar.31	Jun.30	Sep.30	Dec.31	Full Year
1987	.008	.008	.01	.01	.04
1988	.01	.01	.015	.015	.05
1989	.015	.015	.02	.02	.07
1990	.02	.02	.025	.025	.09
1991	.025	.025	.025	.025	

BUSINESS: Circuit City Stores, Inc. is a specialty retailer of video equipment, appliances, audio equipment, and other consumer electronics products. Company operates out of 219 retail locations, mainly in California, Nevada, Southeast, Texas, and mid-Atlantic. Stores include 12 audio and electronics outlets under the name "Circuit City", 176 audio, electronics and appliance stores under the name "Circuit City Superstores", and 31 mall stores under the name "Impulse". Depts. in Zodys discount stores closed 4/86. '90 deprec. rate: 6.6%. Has 5,200 stockholders, 15,000 employees. Insiders own 4.9% of stock. Chairman: Alan L. Wurtzel. President & C.E.O.: Richard L. Sharp. Incorporated: Virginia. Address: 9950 Mayland Drive, Richmond, Virginia 23233. Tel.: 804-527-4000.

Circuit City should post favorable year-to-year earnings comparisons for the second half of fiscal 1991 (ends February 29, 1992). Certainly, the retailer's matchups will be against easy comparisons. But beyond that, sales are improving due to Circuit City's store openings, which have been successful this year. The company has added most of its units in three Texas markets (Dallas, Houston, and Austin) that another consumer electronics chain exited earlier this year. In addition, Circuit City is controlling expenses well via productivity gains. For example, it is reducing staffing levels in back-office areas. Accordingly, we believe the expense ratio will be lower this year. Circuit City's credit-card program is now turning a profit, too. This stock is ranked 2 (Above Average) for year-ahead relative performance.
We look for much higher profits in fiscal 1992. Circuit City will reap a full year's sales from the stores that opened in 1991, and we assume that same-store sales will improve as the economy rebounds. The retailer will also add about 30 Superstores next year (some of which will replace existing Circuit City stores).
Circuit City has designed a new prototype for its Superstores. The company's newly opened stores in Houston and Austin have the new format, and it has remodeled its four Cincinnati units. The new prototype devotes a section of the store to office electronics products such as personal computers, software, computer peripherals, fax machines, and copiers. The margins on these items are lower than on consumer electronics merchandise, but office electronics offers good growth potential without much incremental cost. Circuit City might remodel additional Superstores if the format proves successful.
This issue offers above-average price appreciation potential to 1994-96. Prospective new markets in which Circuit City could open Superstores generate several billion dollars a year in industry consumer electronics sales. Office electronics should also provide solid growth as the company further offers these goods. And Circuit City's mall-based Impulse stores offer much potential for expansion; the company can place a store wherever there is a suitable mall.
Paul E. Debbas *November 29, 1991*

(A) Fiscal year ends last day of February of following calendar year. (B) Primary earnings. Excludes loss due to cumulative effect of accounting change: '90, $1.15. Next earnings report due mid-December. (C) Next dividend meeting about December 13. Goes ex dividend about December 23. Approximate dividend payment dates: January 15, April 15, July 15, October 15. '78 dividend is less than 1¢/sh. after stock splits. (D) Includes deferred taxes. In '90: $50.9 mill., $1.10/sh. (E) In millions, adjusted for stock splits. (F) Excludes Impulse stores.

Company's Financial Strength	B++
Stock's Price Stability	20
Price Growth Persistence	90
Earnings Predictability	65

Figure 4.5 Typical entry, *Value Line Investment Survey*. Copyright © 1991 by Value Line Publishing, Inc. Used by permission.

The Outlook. Standard & Poor's Corp. Weekly.

Unlike the preceding comprehensive survey sources, *The Outlook* is solely concerned with giving investment advice on a few selected companies and industries. Background data is minimal, as analysis of future prospects is the primary focus.

Value Line may be the best place to begin, but look at the other sources for contrasting evaluations and coverage of additional companies.

Brokerage Reports

Closely related to investment advisory reports are brokerage reports. The research departments of large investment and brokerage firms employ analysts, who are experts in their area, to monitor industries and their companies. They follow corporate performance, know many of the industry's top executives, keep in touch with rumors, and are adept at spotting trends. Reports based on their knowledge are sent to local brokerage offices to advise and inform the staff. Most reports are brief, but some are lengthy and may survey competing companies with comments on market share and competitive strategies.

Brokerage reports are seldom available in libraries, for they are intended as in-house publications. If you would like a copy of a specific report, you may request one directly from a broker; however, it is difficult to know what might be available on a particular corporation and from which brokerage firm. An alternative is:

Investext. Thomson Financial Networks. Weekly updates.

An electronic source containing the full text of current reports from many investment banks and research firms. Though widely available as an online database, *Investext* can be an expensive source of information. It is also available as a compact disc product and, in this format, may be available without charge in some very large libraries.

Access to the opinions of financial brokers and analysts is also possible through this publication:

The Wall Street Transcript. The Wall Street Transcript Corp. Weekly.

> Transcripts of roundtable discussions among leading financial analysts within a particular industry are the primary feature of each issue of this weekly financial newspaper. Reprints of selected investment reports, company news releases, and speeches by top corporate executives may also appear. Segments of larger industries that get little coverage in other sources are often examined in detail here. Each issue also profiles three chief executives from the industries under discussion. The *TWST,* as it is known, can be confusing to a first-time user, but its inside information can illuminate the less publicized aspects of a corporation's performance and objectives.

If you cannot access any brokerage report sources, do not despair. Noteworthy investment advice from these reports usually makes its way into *The Wall Street Journal, Barron's,* and other popular financial publications. Gaining access to company information in such sources is your next step.

Use investment advisory publications for information about:

- Financial Data
- Company Strategies
- Industry Outlook

PERIODICAL AND NEWSPAPER ARTICLES

When you study a company as a prospective employer, you want current information. Directories and other books, no matter how recently published, will always be somewhat dated. For the most up-to-date information, turn to periodicals and newspapers.

Hundreds of business periodicals are published. Some are broad in scope, such as *Business Week, Fortune Magazine,* and *Forbes,* and cover both the general economy and specific companies and industries. These are available in almost every library. Others are trade journals, such as *Turkey World, Pit and Quarry,* and *Hardware Age.* Trade journals are highly specialized and devoted to a specific industry or profession. Public and academic libraries subscribe to only a few of these, but a corporation with its own special library may have many trade journals covering its own interests. A growing number of regional business publications are also available, such as *California Business, Corporate Report Minnesota,* and *Toledo Business Journal.* Regional publications cover local companies and business people and survey local and state economy. Libraries often carry the regional business publications of their area. Newspapers, too, contain a great deal of current business information, particularly *The Wall Street Journal,* which is devoted almost solely to business. Other daily newspapers also have extensive business sections.

As you research a company, you want to survey all these publication types for information. You might begin by scanning the last few months of the leading trade journals related to the company's product, the regional business magazine in the company's local area, and two or three general business periodicals or newspapers. Although you may or may not learn anything specific about a company, you will learn something of the primary industry, the regional outlook, and major events on the national business scene. This approach helps you learn about a company's environment—its industry, locality, and national setting. This is a time-consuming method, however, and you may miss relevant articles in other publications. An alternative is to use indexes to business periodicals and newspapers to identify those articles of special interest to you from among the thousands published every year. Choose only those articles directly related to a company, plus any additional general articles you want to scan for background.

Periodical Indexes

Libraries have a variety of indexes to business periodicals; many more are available as online databases. Here are four of the most helpful ones:

Business Periodicals Index. H. W. Wilson Co. Monthly.

If a library has only one business index, it is likely to be this one. Covering approximately 350 English-language periodicals, the subject index encompasses all business topics from accounting to transportation. Company names, industries, products, people—any of these can be used as a starting point for finding an article. General and scholarly business periodicals as well as some trade journals are indexed. *BPI*'s strengths are the quality of its indexing and its thorough coverage of general business and management developments. Its chief drawback is a lack of currency. Articles indexed are sometimes several months old. If currency is very important to you, you will want to supplement *BPI* with another index. *BPI* may be available as a compact disc or an online database in some libraries (see Figure 4.6).

Predicasts F&S Index United States. Predicasts, Inc. Weekly.

An excellent index for current information on U.S. companies, products, and industries, *F&S* covers a wide selection of trade magazines, business-oriented newspapers, financial publications, and special reports. Divided into two sections, Part One

Rainbow Navigation, Inc.

Rainbow loses a round [Rainbow Navigation Company in its fight with the Navy over the carriage of defense cargo to and from Iceland] J. Bonney. *Am Shipp* 32:84 O '90

Rainwater, Richard E.

Rainwater is betting on used cars [Urcarco Inc.] S. Taub. tab *Financ World* 160:12 Je 11 '91

Ralphs Grocery Company

Grocer is sold on self-administration [Ralphs' workers compensation and general liability plans] M. Schachner. *Bus Insur* 25:13 Jl 29 '91

Ralston Purina Co.

Dogged determination: Ralston, cable net make value-added come to life [Ralston Purina's Lucky Dog brand spokesdog appearing in Family Channel programs] A. Fahey. *Advert Age* 62:S22 Jl 22 '91

James Elsesser of Ralston Purina: buyback specialist [chief financial officer] por *Inst Investor* 25:104 Je '91

Thomas ruling shows support of advertising [acceptance of commercial speech in Alpo Petfoods and Ralston Purina deceptive advertising case] S. W. Colford. por *Advert Age* 62:4 Jl 8 '91

Figure 4.6 Typical entries, *Business Periodicals Index,* October 1991 issue. Copyright © 1991 by The H. W. Wilson Company. Reproduced with permission of the publisher.

contains industry and product information arranged by a numeric code based on Standard Industrial Classification (SIC) numbers. Part Two has company information arranged alphabetically by company name, as the example shows. *F&S* may also be available in some libraries as a compact disc or an on-line database (see Figure 4.7).

Business Index. Information Access Co. Monthly.

This index is available on microfilm or as a compact disc; it does not appear in paper. It includes the five most recent years of information in one alphabetic sequence and covers over 800 periodicals. It is convenient, easy to use, and articles are indexed on a timely basis. This index is a good starting point, but subject headings are sometimes inconsistent. Use additional indexes to be sure of finding all pertinent articles. In some

Tandy
To pay former employees $16 mil in back vacation pay. CA
CompResell 04/15/91 p24
Introduces several products in development PC Week 04/08/91 p127
Announces PC, multimedia and CD-ROM plans InfoWEEK 04/08/91 p19
To unveil a new PC line which creates photograph-quality images
WSJ (NJ) 05/03/91 pB4
To roll out 5 new PCs with multimedia capabilities Info Wld 05/06/91 p1
New CDR-1000 is a lower-cost CD-ROM drive Computrwld 03/18/91 p101
Takes stab at multimedia; new line features compact disc/ROM drive Computrwld 05/13/91 p6
Its 286-based notebook PC is reviewed, rated & compared to 10 others Info Wld 05/06/91 p59
Radio Shack distributes this co's personal computer for home, small bsns HFD 04/01/91 p79
Personal computer made by this co to be marketed by Digital Equipment NY Times N 05/15/91 pC5
To perform high-volume portable computer mfg Elec News 04/29/91 p11
Plans to expand Edge in Electronics stores HFD 04/15/91 p230

Tang Industries
Ranks among top Chicago private cos by 1989 revenues. IL (table) ChicagoBTL 00/00/91 p1

Tangram Systems
To unveil AM:PM module for Arbiter PC Week 05/06/91 p41

Figure 4.7 Typical entries, *Predicasts F&S Index United States*, no. 6, 1991. Reprinted by permission of Predicasts, Inc.

libraries, *Business Index* may be part of *Infotrac,* a compact disc system including several indexes.

ABI/Inform. University Microforms, Inc. Monthly.

Available only as a compact disc or an online database, this index has no paper equivalent. Like the previous indexes, it is a subject index covering several hundred business and management periodicals. Its special feature is abstracts, or summaries, of the articles covered. The abstracts outline the main points of an article and can help you decide if you want to read the entire article. The compact disc version of *ABI/Inform* covers only the most recent five years.

These four periodical indexes are the best known and most widely available. There will be considerable overlap among them, but each will list some unique articles. To be thorough, check all of them. If you are going to check only one, the *F&S Index* is known for its excellent coverage of companies and products.

Newspaper Indexes

You will want to read any articles about a company that might have appeared recently in *The Wall Street Journal,* the nation's leading business newspaper. It has its own index:

The Wall Street Journal Index. University Microfilms Inc. Monthly.

Appearing monthly, the index is divided into two parts: Part One is devoted to corporate news listed by company name; Part Two has general news arranged by subject.

Feature articles from *The Wall Street Journal* are also indexed in the *Predicasts F&S Index, Business Index,* and in several online databases.

If you are particularly interested in newspaper coverage of a company, consult other daily newspapers in addition to

The Wall Street Journal. Many of these have extensive business sections, and the large ones such as the *New York Times* and *Washington Post* also have their own indexes. If your library subscribes to a nationally distributed newspaper, the indexes may also be available.

Don't overlook the local or regional newspapers in the area where a company is located. News items that rate only a brief mention, or none at all, in national newspapers may get full coverage in a company's hometown newspaper. Indexing for smaller newspapers is less likely to be widely available, although electronic access is increasing.

Trade Journals

Trade journals have been mentioned several times, but how can you identify those for the industry you are considering? Several directories of periodicals are available; the best known are:

Ulrich's International Periodicals Directory. R. R. Bowker. Annual.

The Standard Periodical Directory. Oxbridge Communications, Inc. Annual.

Gale Directory of Publications and Broadcast Media. Gale Research Inc. Annual.

> Arrangement differs somewhat in each but all provide broad subject access. If it is available, *Ulrich's* may be a good first choice to consult. As the example shows, this directory generally notes if a periodical is indexed and where (see Figure 4.8).

How can you find relevant articles in trade journals? Only those with very wide readership or coverage of major industries will be covered in the four indexes mentioned earlier. The best option for using the highly specialized trade journals is to browse through issues for the past several months. Read any articles that mention the company you are researching and scan others for a sense of trends in the industry.

664.028 658.8 US ISSN 0016-2191
HD9001 CODEN: FFOADT

FROZEN FOOD AGE; the industry magazine of marketing and merchandising. 1952. m. $35. Frozen Food Age Publishing Corp., 230 Park Ave., New York, NY 10017. TEL 212-697-4627. FAX 212-599-2653. Ed. Duane D. Shelton. adv. charts, illus. stat. circ. 18,000. (tabloid format) Indexed: Int. Packag. Abstr. Ref. Pt. Food Indus. Abstr.

664.028 US ISSN 0889-5902
TP493.5.A1 CODEN: FFDIEX

FROZEN FOOD DIGEST; the informative magazine of the frozen food industry. 1985. 4/yr. $26. Frozen Food Digest, Inc., 271 Madison Ave., New York, NY 10016. TEL 212-557-8600. FAX 212-986-9868. Eds. Jim McGinness, Faye Louis. adv. bk. rev. circ. 15,000. Indexed: Tr. & Indus. Ind.

664.028 US

FROZEN FOOD EXECUTIVE. 1983. m. $60. National Frozen Food Association, Inc., Box 6069, Harrisburg, PA 17112-0069. TEL 717-657-8601. FAX 717-657-9862. Ed. Cindi Griggs Rockwell. adv. stat. circ. 4,142. (back issues avail.)

Description: News about the frozen food industry with information on NFFA, new products, legislation and statistics.

Figure 4.8 Typical entries, *Ulrich's International Periodicals Directory*. Copyright © 1991, by Reed Publishing (USA) Inc; reprinted with permission of R. R. Bowker, a division of Reed Publishing (USA) Inc.

Online Database Indexes

If you are unable to find information in any other way, consider an online database search. Information in online databases is sometimes difficult to obtain elsewhere and may be more current than that found in print sources. A growing number of business databases, many of them providing access to highly specialized periodicals, are available. Some databases simply index publications; others offer an abstract or even the full text of articles.

Many libraries provide online services but charge a fee to cover costs from the database vendor. Ask at your library about available databases and the estimated cost to have one of them searched for information about a company. As business databases are among the most expensive offered, be prepared to pay a sizable fee for this kind of information. Read more about online database access in Chapter 12.

If you search widely for articles, especially in online databases, you may have difficulty obtaining the periodicals cited. No single library may have everything you want, particularly if you are seeking trade journals with a narrow audience. If you have started your research well ahead of any deadlines, your library may be able to obtain copies of the articles from another library through the process called "interlibrary loan." It usually takes 10 to 20 days for this service, and libraries often charge a modest fee for copying and handling. Some libraries may provide rush service by telefacsimile for an additional fee.

Use periodical and newspaper articles for information about:

- Facilities
- Company Size
- Product/Service
- Financial Data
- Company History
- Company Strategies
- Response to Difficulty
- Management/Employee Data
- Executive Biography
- Employee Morale
- Salaries
- Industry Outlook

BIOGRAPHICAL SOURCES FOR TOP EXECUTIVES

The background of a company's executives can provide a clue to the training and experience valued by the company. It may also suggest items to highlight in your resume. Information about top executives in large national firms is fairly easy to locate, but executives of smaller firms may be more difficult to find. Information about middle managers, even their names, may be impossible to determine unless you have a contact within the company.

The national business directories noted earlier in this chapter usually list the names and titles of the top executives of each company. Large firms may identify 20 or 30 individuals; smaller firms only one or two. One of those directories,

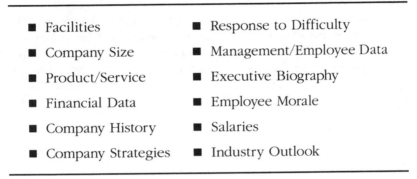

Standard & Poor's Register of Corporations, Directors, and Executives, devotes a volume to executive biography. Volume two contains brief biographies of about 25 percent of the directors and officers of the corporations included in the main directory volume. Another source of biographical information for top executives is a corporation's 10-K report, which usually identifies top management and, in some circumstances, includes their background, company stock holdings, and compensation.

For additional information about top corporate executives, check one of these directories:

Reference Book of Corporate Management. Dun & Bradstreet Information Services. Annual.

> This multivolume set is arranged by company name and contains entries for 12,000 companies, with brief biographies of their top executives and directors. Included are date of birth, education, an employment history, and the position currently held. If the compact disc product *Duns Million Dollar Disc* is available in your library, this biographical data is included (see Figure 4.9).

Who's Who in Finance and Industry. Marquis Who's Who. Biennial.

> This directory contains career sketches of over 20,000 leading business executives in the United States and Canada. Each profile contains personal data, education, career history, political or civic affiliations, and special achievements.

If searching for executives of less well-known firms, the following set may be worth a try:

Biography and Genealogy Master Index. Gale Research Inc. Annual.

> This is an index to hundreds of published sources of collective biography, covering individuals in all fields of endeavor. The scope of the biographical sources analyzed is very broad, but most individuals included are of some national prominence. The index is also available as an online database.

D-U-N-S 99 265 8824
MINNESOTA CASUALTY COMPANY (INC)
MCC Plaza
Minneapolis, MN 55402

SIC 6321 *TEL* (612) 222-4567
Insurance

CH PR*—NOLAN, THOMAS J. b. 1927; m; grad Northwestern BSBA: 1950-1954 USN, Lt(jg); 1955-1962 Dept of Justice; 1962-1965 Better Life Ins Co; 1965-1970 Howard Co, sr exec off; 1970-present Minnesota Casualty Company, chmn bd, pres & chief exec off; dir.

SR VP*—EDWARDS, LAWRENCE T, b. 1935; m; 1957 Drake Univ BS; 1962-1975 Howard Co, vp; 1975-present Minnesota Casualty Company, 1975 sr vp-mktg, 1977 sr vp-central opns; dir.

SR VP—MARTIN, STEPHEN M, b. 1927; m; 1952 Univ of Penn BS; 1950-present Minnesota Casualty Company, 1950 underwriter, 1957 asst sec, 1959 asst vp, 1964 asst to pres, 1965 vp, 1974 sr vp-reins, 1977 sr vp specialty opns.

SR VP—WHITMAN, CHARLES R, b. 1923; m; 1948 Univ of Minn BS; yrs to present Minnesota Casualty Company, 1969 vp, 1974 sr vp.

SR VP*—WILE, WILLIAM V, b. 1919; m; Univ of Penn; 1942-1945 US Army, Capt; 1946-1947 Sidney, Endle & Co; 1948-1949 Smith & Co, acct exec; 1949-1955 St Elmo Ins Co, br mgr; 1955-present Minnesota Casualty Company, 1961 asst vp-eastern & central regs, then asst vp & br mgr, 1970 vp & reg dir-eastern reg, 1975 vp & reg dir-southern reg, 1977 sr vp-field opns home off; dir.

TR—HALLECK, THOMAS J, b. 1943, 1962 Univ of Iowa MA; 1963-1967 USAF, Capt; 1967-1968 Export Bank of Des Moines, project budget analyst; 1970-present Minnesota Casualty Company, 1971 asst treas, 1973 treas.

Figure 4.9 Typical entry, *Reference Book of Corporate Management.* Copyright 1992 by Dun & Bradstreet Inc. All rights reserved. Reprinted by permission.

If the executives you are searching for are not in these sources, personal contacts may provide the best source of information.

COMPANY HISTORY

Usually, you can find the basic facts of a company's history in the directories and financial sources already described in this chapter. The founding date and important merger dates are easy to determine. But what else happened in a company's past and who was the company founder? These facts may not be particularly significant today, but they can help you understand the traditions and attitudes that underlie the company's ethos.

Start a search for company history in your library's catalog. If a full book has been written and is in your library's collection, it should be listed under the company name as a subject; try that first. Should that fail, look for a history of the company's industry; a general study may include details of the company's background. Don't be surprised if you come up empty handed. Few companies rate full histories, and a library may carry only those of major corporations or those of local interest. If available, try this quick guide to recent company histories:

Wahib Nasrallah. *United States Corporation Histories: a Bibliography 1965–1990,* 2nd ed. Garland. 1991.

> The histories of corporations found in books, articles, pamphlets, and academic theses during a 25-year period are covered by this guide. All are listed by company name.

If you identify a history that is not available in your library, you may be able to obtain it through the library's interlibrary loan service, but allow at least two to three weeks for this.

Lacking a full-length book, look for history as you scan periodical and newspaper articles. Note facts as you find them and compile your own history of important dates and events in the company's past. Also, several books that give brief profiles of major corporations, including history, have been published in the past decade. Try these for short histories. One of the best known is:

Milton Moskowitz, Robert Levering, and Michael Katz. *Everybody's Business: A Field Guide to the 400 Leading Companies in America.* Doubleday. 1990.

> This readable survey of top corporations describes firms from an informal perspective. In addition to history, each brief company profile may include rankings of products and services, brand names, executives and major owners, workplace environment, international presence, social consciousness, and stock performance.

PRODUCT AND SERVICES INFORMATION

Several sources discussed previously contain product and service information. Every directory mentions the major business lines or product areas of a company. One of the major national directories noted earlier in this chapter, *Thomas Register of American Manufacturers,* includes company product catalogs and advertisements for manufacturers in several of its volumes as well as a list of brand names. Annual reports and 10-K reports specify some product and brand data. Periodical and newspaper articles are a good source of product information, especially for new products and major national brands. The *Predicasts F&S Index,* mentioned earlier, is particularly useful in tracking product stories.

You may be able to answer some questions about products and brands simply by observation. For example, retail prices of consumer products are easy to discover—just visit or call a store that sells the product. Visiting the store is preferable, because you can compare the prices on competing brands while you are there. Look at the product to judge its quality, too, and ask a salesperson how brands compare in terms of customer satisfaction. Bear in mind these will be subjective opinions.

If you want an independent judgment of a brand, look for a consumer product rating. Several periodicals carry articles that compare brands; one of the best known is *Consumer Reports.* This magazine and others with similar articles are indexed in:

Consumers Index to Product Evaluations and Information Sources. The Pierian Press Inc. Quarterly.

> About 100 general interest, hobby, and consumer magazines are indexed for articles on products, health, and money-saving ideas. A code indicates whether the article describes, evaluates, or tests a particular product or brand. Indexes by company name and product name are included.

If you have difficulty determining the brand names used by a corporation, try this directory:

Brands and Their Companies/Companies and Their Brands. Gale Research Inc. Annual.

The *Brands* volume lists nearly 230,000 trade names, trademarks, and brand names and identifies the company that manufactures or distributes each item. The *Companies* volume presents the same names, but lists them alphabetically by company.

Judging the competitive price and quality of industrial products will be more difficult. Wholesale distributors are a possible source of information. They serve as salespersons to industrial or retail customers. Identify a brand's local distributor by checking the yellow pages of the telephone book. When you call or visit a distributor, explain that you are not a potential customer and make the purpose of your questions clear.

The purchaser of an industrial product, the distributor's or the manufacturer's direct customer, is also in a position to judge the quality and price of a product. If you can determine the identity of such customers, they may be willing to offer an opinion of a product's value and quality.

If the company you are evaluating provides a service rather than a product, the price and quality of the service may also prove difficult and time consuming to compare with that of a competitor. A user or purchaser of the service may be best placed to comment on its relative value and quality. Your approach to obtaining this information may depend on the service. Judge how necessary this is to your evaluation of the company before alloting time and creativity to the search.

INDUSTRY ANALYSES

An acquaintance with the industry represented by a company is essential to fully understand and evaluate a firm. Knowledge of the industry sets the stage by outlining the current situation that faces competing companies. It also illuminates a firm's future by considering the general outlook. Don't skip this step—your long-term opportunities in a good company may be markedly affected if it is part of a declining, rather than a stable or even a booming, industry.

Industry analysis appears in several sources, some already noted. For example, periodical articles frequently survey an entire industry. Trade journals, in particular, may provide year-end summary reviews of events and trends within the industry they cover. Forecast issues are also common in trade journals. The *Value Line Investment Survey,* mentioned earlier, includes two- to three-page overviews of the 90 industry groups it profiles, updated every quarter. The brokers' analyses in *The Wall Street Transcript* also provide commentary on industry conditions.

Industrial Surveys

Two publications, available in many libraries, focus specifically on industrywide reports. They are:

Standard & Poor's Industry Surveys. Standard & Poor's Corp. Annual with quarterly updates.

> This is a valuable source of basic data and outlook commentary for approximately 25 broad industry categories. A "Basic Analysis" section annually reviews the status of several industry segments within each category. Graphs and tables as well as summary financial data for the leading companies in each industry segment are included. A "Current Analysis" section, updated quarterly, provides an interim review for each of the broad categories.

U.S. Industrial Outlook. U.S. Department of Commerce. Annual.

> The U.S. government publishes this survey of current trends and outlook for about 350 industries. Individual companies are not mentioned, but the industry data and projections include useful information about changes in supply and demand, developments in domestic and foreign markets, employment trends, and capital investment, as well as statistics drawn from U.S. census data.

Industry Averages

If you are particularly interested in the financial performance of the company you are considering as an employer, compare its performance with others in the same industry by looking at a company's financial ratios in comparison with industrywide ratios. Ratios are derived from the percentage relationship between certain pairs of figures drawn from a firm's financial statement. Examining the ratios reveals the strengths and weaknesses of a company's financial situation, and comparing the figures with industry ratios or averages shows the company's competitive financial position. Several sources for industry ratios are published; many are highly specialized and not widely available. Two of the best known and most frequently found in libraries are:

RMA Annual Statement Studies. Robert Morris Associates. Annual.

> This well-known and respected source of financial ratios published by an association of bank loan officers contains broad industry breakdowns for over 350 manufacturing, wholesaling, and retailing categories, plus selected service and construction industries. Data for each industry are presented in four asset-size groups so that companies can be compared with others of equal size. Balance sheet and income data averages are also provided for each industry group.

Industry Norms and Key Business Ratios. Dun & Bradstreet Information Services. Annual.

> Available in various formats, this volume provides up to three years of industry financial statistics on over 800 lines of business. Arranged by Standard Industrial Classification (SIC) codes, the common size percentages for each industry are presented in balance sheet format divided into median, upper, and lower quartiles. The 14 ratios characterize solvency, efficiency, and profitability.

Before you compare a company with the ratios for its industry, remember that ratio analysis is a fairly complex task, requiring some knowledge of financial principles. If you are not sure what the figures mean, get some help with the interpretation from an experienced source.

Business Rankings

Another form of comparison between companies in an industry is business rankings. Rankings are increasingly popular and are found in many publications. While companies are ranked by a wide variety of factors, sales and number of employees are the most commonly used. Periodicals such as *Business Week, Forbes,* and *Fortune Magazine* are known for their ranked lists. The "Fortune 500," published in the periodical of that name each spring and widely known for its ranking of the largest industrial companies, is only one example. Some directories, most notably *Ward's Business Directory of U.S. Private and Public Companies* mentioned earlier in this chapter, also contain ranked lists. A volume of *Ward's* ranks companies within industry categories by sales. It also has ranked lists of the largest public and private companies.

Business rankings are a speciality of these two publications:

Dun's Business Rankings. Dun & Bradstreet Information Services. Annual.

> Listings include 25,000 major companies ranked by sales and by number of employees nationally, within state, SIC categories, public and private company designations.

Business Rankings Annual. Gale Research Inc. Annual.

> This volume is an index to business rankings that appear in periodicals, newspapers, directories, and statistical publications. In addition to citing the original source of each ranked list and the criteria for the ranking, the top 10 names in each list are given. An index of company names and industries will lead you to rankings including a specific company.

Trade Associations

Trade associations are an important source of industry information. Most industries have an association that promotes products, gathers statistics, educates the public, lobbies legislatures, and ensures that industry interests are not overlooked. The number and variety of trade associations at the national level is staggering. Regional and local trade associations are equally numerous. Information gathering and dissemination is a key role for most of these associations. While some extend services only to members, many are willing and even eager to share information about their industry with the public. To determine if a trade association has been established for an industry, try this directory:

Encyclopedia of Associations. Gale Research Inc. Annual.

> A guide to national and international organizations of the United States, including 4,000 trade and industry associations. Each entry includes an address, telephone number, and contact name. Staff and membership numbers are indicated, along with a statement describing the organization's purpose and its publications. A keyword index helps to determine the relevant associations for an industry.

Call or write the appropriate association asking for information to help evaluate the industry and company you are considering as an employer. For the best and most useful responses, make your questions brief and specific.

Use industry analyses for information about:

- Company Size
- Product/Services
- Financial Data
- Industry Outlook

Although nearly all the suggested sources for publicly owned companies are available in libraries and information centers, don't assume that the library is the only place to look. Many other possibilities exist; they are particularly important for private companies or very small companies but can also be useful for publicly owned firms. Personal contacts may also be helpful in revealing many aspects of publicly owned corporations.

Chapters 7 and 8 provide ideas for additional research possibilities beyond the library.

Use sources outside the library for information about:

- Facilities
- Company Strategies
- Response to Difficulty
- Management/Employee Data
- Executive Biography
- Employee Morale
- Salaries
- Industry Outlook

5 Researching Subsidiaries and Divisions of Publicly Owned Companies

A corporation may consist of separate subordinate units known as subsidiaries or divisions. These units are often more difficult to research than the corporation as a whole, because information about them is less complete than for the units' parent company. The primary focus of this chapter will be the subsidiaries of publicly owned companies (see Figure 5.1). If the company you are researching is a subsidiary of a privately held corporation or a foreign-owned firm, you will find further information in Chapters 6 and 7.

DIRECTORIES

A directory provides basic facts about a company—location, number of employees, annual sales, top executives. Those that list subsidiaries are no exception. Directories that helped to

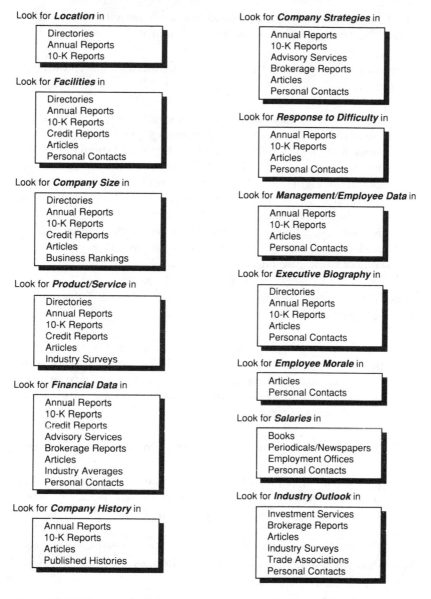

Look for ***Location*** in

- Directories
- Annual Reports
- 10-K Reports

Look for ***Facilities*** in

- Directories
- Annual Reports
- 10-K Reports
- Credit Reports
- Articles
- Personal Contacts

Look for ***Company Size*** in

- Directories
- Annual Reports
- 10-K Reports
- Credit Reports
- Articles
- Business Rankings

Look for ***Product/Service*** in

- Directories
- Annual Reports
- 10-K Reports
- Credit Reports
- Articles
- Industry Surveys

Look for ***Financial Data*** in

- Annual Reports
- 10-K Reports
- Credit Reports
- Advisory Services
- Brokerage Reports
- Articles
- Industry Averages
- Personal Contacts

Look for ***Company History*** in

- Annual Reports
- 10-K Reports
- Articles
- Published Histories

Look for ***Company Strategies*** in

- Annual Reports
- 10-K Reports
- Advisory Services
- Brokerage Reports
- Articles
- Personal Contacts

Look for ***Response to Difficulty*** in

- Annual Reports
- 10-K Reports
- Articles
- Personal Contacts

Look for ***Management/Employee Data*** in

- Annual Reports
- 10-K Reports
- Articles
- Personal Contacts

Look for ***Executive Biography*** in

- Directories
- Annual Reports
- 10-K Reports
- Articles
- Personal Contacts

Look for ***Employee Morale*** in

- Articles
- Personal Contacts

Look for ***Salaries*** in

- Books
- Periodicals/Newspapers
- Employment Offices
- Personal Contacts

Look for ***Industry Outlook*** in

- Investment Services
- Brokerage Reports
- Articles
- Industry Surveys
- Trade Associations
- Personal Contacts

Figure 5.1 Research checklist for a subsidiary or division.

identify a company as a subsidiary also provide basic facts about the firms. Look briefly at them again:

Directory of Corporate Affiliations. National Register Publishing Co. Annual.

> As many as 40,000 divisions, subsidiaries, and affiliates are listed in this directory, which provides the headquarters address, telephone number, line of business, and the name of the unit's top officer for each of the separate corporate entities, as shown in Figure 5.2. Sales and employee numbers are also given for each, if available. The percentage of ownership may be indicated. Although most of the companies listed are publicly owned, a few of the largest private companies are also included. The directory is also available as an online database or compact disc (see Figure 5.2).

America's Corporate Families. Dun & Bradstreet Information Services. Annual.

> The 67,000 U.S. subsidiaries, divisions, and major branches in this directory are identified with address, top executives, business or product lines, and the name of the parent corporation. When available, sales and number of employees are also noted; 11,000 parent companies are listed.

Who Owns Whom. Dun & Bradstreet International. Annual.

> This directory shows only the corporate ownership structure and the subsidiary company's country of incorporation. When available, the percentage of ownership is indicated.

The first two of these directories have considerable overlap; however, each has some unique listings. If both are available, check both for information.

Look also at the national business directories suggested in the preceding chapter. In addition to major public corporations, the national directories list and provide data for many of the larger subsidiaries and divisions. Subsidiary status is generally noted. Also, don't overlook specialized directories, particularly the state industrial directories, described in Chapter 4. The

• 7095-000
DAYTON HUDSON CORPORATION
777 Nicollet Mall
Minneapolis, MN 55402
Tel.: 612-370-6948 **MN**
Telefax: 612-375-3058
DH—(NYSE PS)
Assets: $6,075,500,000
Earnings: $410,000,000
Liabilities: $4,089,500,000
Net Worth: $1,986,000,000
Approx. Rev.: $13,644,000,000
Emp: 120,000
Fiscal Year-end: 2/3/90
National Diversified Retailer;
Department Stores; Books
S.I.C.: 5942; 5331; 5946; 5311
Kenneth A. Macke *(Cbm. Bd. & Chief Exec. Officer)*
Stephen E. Watson *(Pres.)*
James T. Hale *(Sr. V.P., Gen. Counsel & Sec.)*
Willard C. Shull III *(Sr. V.P.-Fin.)*
Edwin H. Wingate *(Sr. V.P.-Personnel)*
Ann H. Barkelew *(V.P.-Pub. Rels.)*
Larry E. Carlson *(V.P.)*
Karol D. Emmerich *(V.P. & Treas.)*
L. Fred Hamacher *(V.P.)*
William E. Harder *(V.P. & Asst. Sec.)*
Peter Hutchinson *(V.P.)*
James R. Eckmann *(Asst. Treas.)*
William P. Hise *(Asst. Sec.)*

Board of Directors:
Kenneth A. Macke
Rand V. Araskog
Robert A. Burnett
Livio D. DeSimone
Roger L. Hale
Donald J. Hall
Betty Ruth Hollander
David T. Kearns
Howard H. Kehrl
Bruce K. MacLaury
David T. McLaughlin
John A. Rollwagen
Boake A. Sells
Stephen E. Watson
Shirley Young

4630-000
Faegre & Benson *(Legal Firm)*
2200 Norwest Ctr., 90 S. 7th St.
Minneapolis, MN 55402-3901
Tel.: 612-336-3000

28223-000
First Chicago Trust Company of New York *(Transfer Agent)*
30 W. Broadway

Divisions:

7085-002
Dayton Hudson Department Store Company (1)
700 Nicollet Mall
Minneapolis, MN 55402
Tel.: 612-375-2200
Telefax: 612-375-3340
Approx. Sls.: $1,552,300,000
Emp: 25,000
Fiscal Year-end: 12/31/89
Department Stores
Mervin Goldstein *(Cbm. Bd. & Pres.)*

Regions:

7085-008
Hudson's-Region 1 (2)
21500 Northwestern Hwy.
Southfield, MI 48075
Tel.: 313-443-6000
Department Stores

7085-010
Dayton's-Region 2 (2)
700 Nicollet Mall
Minneapolis, MN 55402
Tel.: 612-375-2200
Telefax: 612-375-3340
Department Store
S.I.C.: 5311

7085-005
Target Stores (1)
33 S. 6th St.
Minneapolis, MN 55440 (MN)
Mailing Address: P.O. Box 1392
Minneapolis, MN 55440
Tel.: 612-370-6073 (100%)
Telefax: 612-370-8309
Approx. Sls.: $5,306,100,000
Emp: 56,600
Fiscal Year-end: 12/31/89
Discount & Hard Goods Store
S.I.C.: 5331
Robert J. Ulrich *(Cbm. & Chief Exec. Officer)*
Warren Feldberg *(Exec. V.P.-Mdsg.)*
George Jones *(Exec. V.P.-Store Opers.)*

Subsidiaries:

7085-012
Marshall Field & Co. (1)
111 N. State St.
Chicago, IL 60602 (DE)
Tel.: 312-781-1000 (100%)
Telefax: 312-781-3011
Approx. Sls.: $1,000,000,000
Emp: 15,000
Fiscal Year-end: 12/31/89
Operates 25 Department Stores in Illinois, Texas & Wisconsin
S.I.C.: 5311
Gary Witkin *(Pres.)*
Michael MacDonald *(Sr. V.P. & Chief Fin. Officer)*
Christina Johnson-Wolff *(Sr. V.P. & Gen. Mdse. Mgr.-Direct Response & Home Store)*
Kathy Wickstrom *(Sr. V.P.-Reg. Stores)*
P. Johnson *(Sr. V.P.-Personnel)*
W.G. Brown *(Sr. V.P.-Opers.)*
Kassie Davis *(Dir.-Pub. Affairs)*

7085-008
Mervyn's (1)
25001 Industrial Blvd.
Hayward, CA 94545 (CA)
Tel.: 415-785-8800 (100%)
Telefax: 415-785-8906
Approx. Sls.: $3,182,600,000
Emp: 44,600
Soft Goods Department Store
S.I.C.: 5311
Walter T. Rossi *(Cbm. & Chief Exec. Officer)*
Joseph C. Veece *(Pres. & Chief Oper. Officer)*
7097-000

Figure 5.2 Typical entry, *Directory of Corporate Affiliations,* 1991 edition. Published by National Register Publishing Co., a division of Reed Reference Publishing Company. Used by permission.

scope of these directories allows the inclusion of many smaller companies, divisions, and branch locations. Remember, too, that specialized directories may include details not found elsewhere.

Use directories for information about:

- Location
- Facilities
- Company Size
- Product/Service
- Executive Biography

FINANCIAL REPORTS AND STATEMENTS

Financial data for publicly owned corporations is widely available because the companies are required to report their financial status to their stockholders and to the U.S. Securities and Exchange Commission (SEC). However, publicly owned companies are *not* required to provide full financial disclosure for each of the individual units—the subsidiaries and divisions—that make up the corporation. Nor are they required to file a separate annual report and disclosure statement for each of the individual subsidiaries and divisions. Publicly owned companies are only required to provide "segment data" for any line of business that contributes 10 percent or more of the total revenues or assets of the firm. Under this rule, which groups together the data of units producing similar products, it may not be possible to determine exactly how a particular subsidiary or division is performing financially.

For example, if a corporation derives 15 percent of its revenues from a business segment comprising three divisions that manufacture soaps and detergents, it must provide financial data for this line of business in its annual financial report. The data are grouped together for the three units, however, and the individual contribution of each division to the corporation's total performance cannot be determined. On the other hand, the same corporation may have one subsidiary that manufactures toys. If this line of business contributes at least 10 percent of the total corporate revenues, it must be reported as a separate business segment. And, because there is only a single unit in the toys segment, its individual contribution to the company's total performance can be easily ascertained.

The narrative sections of annual reports and disclosure filings often present division and subsidiary information in the same way as the financial portions of the reports. Evaluations of the current corporate situation, its functions and its outlook, are grouped into the same segment or line of business units used for financial reporting. Again, if several subsidiaries and divisions are grouped in these management discussions, it may be difficult to separate out the current standing and future outlook for an individual unit. Read the parent corporation's annual reports and SEC disclosure statements with care. They may provide valuable clues to many aspects of general corporate activity and policy. The section on financial reports in the preceding chapter tells you how to obtain these documents if they are not available in your library. Gather clues from the reports about the unit you are researching. Then verify or explore them in more depth in other resources.

The *Moody's Manuals* and *Standard & Poor's Corporation Records,* mentioned in Chapter 4 as a source of consolidated annual financial data for publicly owned companies, will be of little value in researching individual units of a corporation; they only list the corporate units. The credit reporting services also described in Chapter 4 may include the business segments of a corporation in their evaluations, but the cost of obtaining the reports may make them an impractical option.

Use financial reports and statements for information about:

- Location
- Facilities
- Company Size
- Product/Service
- Financial Data
- Company History
- Company Strategies
- Response to Difficulty
- Management/Employee Data
- Executive Biography

If the subsidiary or division has a privately held parent, remember that annual reports and SEC filings for the parent will not be available. Refer to Chapter 7 for alternative suggestions to determine the financial status of such units. Financial reporting for foreign-owned subsidiaries will also be markedly different. Chapter 6 has some suggestions for locating data about foreign-owned units.

INVESTMENT ADVISORY PUBLICATIONS

Shares of stock in the subsidiaries and divisions of a publicly owned company are not traded on the stock exchanges, only shares of the parent company. Subsidiaries are not listed in the newspaper stock quotations or investment advisory sources as is the parent. However, the success or failure of a business unit can strongly affect the overall fate of a corporation. Investors are often keenly interested in the response of a particular division or subsidiary to economic challenge. Therefore, investment advisory publications frequently comment on the current performance and the outlook for individual business units or entire business segments within the context of the discussion of the parent corporation.

The most commonly available of these investment services are the following: *Value Line Investment Survey* (Value Line, Inc., weekly), *Standard Stock Reports* (Standard & Poor's Corp., quarterly), *Moody's Handbook of Common Stocks* (Moody's Investors Service, quarterly), and *The Outlook* (Standard & Poor's Corp., weekly). All are described in Chapter 4. Just as you use the parent company's annual financial reports for clues, you can read the investment advisory publications' discussions of the parent corporation for the same purpose. Keep in mind, however, that these investment sources present only brief summary comments on a corporation, so that the reference to any individual segment or unit will be succinct and perhaps tangential. Nevertheless, it may indicate the activity within the unit and expectations for future operations.

As an example, look at the way such information is covered in this company profile from *Moody's Handbook of Common Stocks*. Note that divisions and subsidiaries and their effect

CRANE CO.

LISTED	SYM.	LTPS♦	STPS♦	IND. DIV.	REC. PRICE	RANGE (52-WKS.)	YLD.
NYSE	CR	109.4	108.8	$0.75	28	30 - 18	2.7%

MEDIUM GRADE. EARNINGS ARE INFLUENCED BY CAPITAL SPENDING AND GENERAL ECONOMIC CONDITIONS.

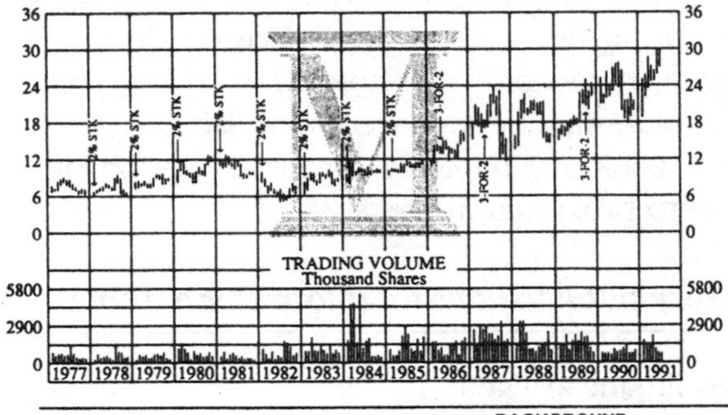

CAPITALIZATION: (12/31/90)

	(000)	(%)
Long-Term Debt.	k$104,143	12.7
Defer. Inc. Tax	49,477	6.1
Com. & Surp.	664,811	81.2
Total	$818,431	100.0

Shs. ($6.25)-31,244,579

INTERIM EARNINGS:

Qtr.	3/31	6/30	9/30	12/31
1987g	0.17	0.41	0.47	0.39
1988e	0.27	0.39	0.41	0.37
1989	0.33	0.49	0.48	0.42
1990	0.42	0.50	0.53	0.51
1991	0.30	0.40	...	...

INTERIM DIVIDENDS:

Amt.	Dec.	Ex.	Rec.	Pay.
0.1875Q	8/20/90	8/29/90	9/5/90	9/14/90
0.1875Q	11/19	11/28	12/4	12/14
0.1875Q	2/25/91	3/4/91	3/8/91	3/14/91
0.1875Q	5/6	5/31	6/6	6/14
0.1875Q	8/26	8/30	9/6	9/13

BACKGROUND:

Crane is a manufacturer of engineered industrial products, seving markets in aerospace, fluid handling, automatic merchandising and the construction industry. Crane's wholesale distribution business serves the building products markets and industrial customers. In 1990, sales (and operating profit) were derived as follows: engineered industrial products, 52% (80%); and wholesale distribution, 48% (20%). Products include industrial fluid control products and systems, handling and launching systems, precision ordinance and related electromechanical and electronic devices, systems and machines for automated production, fiber glass reinforced panels and structured walls, automatic-merchandising equipment, and millwork. Crane Supply Canada is a distributor of industrial supplies and products.

RECENT DEVELOPMENTS:

For the quarter ended 6/30/91, net income dropped 20% to $12.8 million compared with $16.1 million the previous year. Sales declined 11% to $339.2 million. Both of Crane's two business segments reported declines in sales and operating profit primarily due to recessionary conditions in the United States, Canada and the United Kingdom. The decline in the Engineered Industrial Products profit was caused by a loss in the Company's U.K. operations, a decline in sales to the truck trailer transportation market at Kemlite and Cor Tec, and lower margins at Hydro-Aire.

PROSPECTS:

Near-term earnings growth may remain sluggish as the Huttig housing division continues to recover at a sluggish rate. However, the Hydro-Aire subsidiary will benefit from a huge backlog supported by large equipment orders and backlog for Boeing aircraft. Hydro-Aire's parts business is likely to improve as demand for air travel increases. In addition, the aircraft brake parts segment will be enhanced by the increased building rates for new commercial aircraft. Although Canadian operations will continue to be weak, costs will be under control, reducing losses.

STATISTICS:

YEAR	GROSS REVS. ($mill.)	OPER. PROFIT MARGIN %	RET. ON EQUITY %	NET INCOME ($mill.)	WORK CAP. ($mill.)	SENIOR CAPITAL ($mill.)	SHARES (000)	EARN. PER SH.$	DIV. PER SH.$	DIV. PAY. %	PRICE RANGE	P/E RATIO	AVG. YIELD %
81	1,611.3	7.0	17.9	53.8	199.5	277.0	36,738	1.44	0.472	33	13⅜ - 7⅝	7.3	2.4
82	1,126.4	d	—	d3.3	188.8	246.6	35,742	d0.09	0.453	—	10⅛ - 5	—	2.3
b83	771.7	3.3	10.4	a26.4	207.4	202.4	35,154	a0.75	0.579	77	9¾ - 6⅜	10.8	2.9
84	792.2	6.4	14.7	31.0	147.9	138.7	30,455	0.95	0.474	50	11⅞ - 7⅞	10.4	2.4
85	1,098.8	6.4	11.2	c17.6	211.1	275.9	44,202	c0.57	0.385	68	12⅛ - 9½	19.0	1.9
86	1,204.2	7.6	22.2	38.4	188.2	232.1	30,081	1.25	0.567	45	16⅝ - 11	11.1	2.8
87	1,284.0	8.1	23.2	g50.3	184.4	156.3	33,639	g1.43	0.789	55	23⅝ - 11⅝	12.3	3.9
88	1,313.1	7.3	17.9	e49.2	236.7	143.1	32,787	e1.45	0.708	49	22⅝ - 13½	12.5	3.5
89	1,455.6	8.7	8.5	55.9	213.9	119.1	31,808	1.72	0.708	41	25 - 15	11.6	3.5
90	**1,438.2**	**8.6**	**9.4**	**62.7**	**217.8**	**104.1**	**31,245**	**1.96**	**0.75**	**38**	**27¾ - 17¾**	**11.6**	**3.3**

♦Long-Term Price Score — Short-Term Price Score; see page 4a. STATISTICS ARE AS ORIGINALLY REPORTED. Adjusted for all stock splits and dividends through 3-for-2 split, 9/89. a-Excl. a loss from discont. oper. of $135.4 mill., or $d5.79 per sh. b-Continuing operations. c-Reflects after-tax charge of $12.7 mill. related to restructure and closure of certain operations. e-Before. discontinued operations of $13.3 mill. ($0.39 a sh.) g-Before $9.0 million ($0.25 a sh.) accounting adjustment. k-Incl. debentures conv. into com.

INCORPORATED:
May 1985 — DE

PRINCIPAL OFFICE:
757 3rd Avenue
New York, NY 10017
Tel.: (212) 415-7300

ANNUAL MEETING:
In May

NUMBER OF STOCKHOLDERS:
7,900

TRANSFER AGENT(S):
First Chicago Trust Co. of N.Y.
New York, NY

REGISTRAR(S):
First Chicago Trust Co. of N.Y.
New York, NY

INSTITUTIONAL HOLDINGS:
No. of Institutions: 180
Shares Held: 17,873,796

OFFICERS:
Chmn., Pres., C.E.O. &
R. S. Evans
Vice Pres.-Fin & C.F.O.
J. P. Cronin
Vice-Pres. & Sec.
P. R. Hundt

Figure 5.3 Typical entry, *Moody's Handbook of Common Stocks*, Fall 1991. Reprinted by permission of Moody's Investors Service.

on the company's standing are mentioned several times in the narrative (see Figure 5.3).

Brokerage reports, like investment services, focus on the entire corporate unit but, again, the fate of a division or subsidiary can affect the fortunes of the whole. If relevant, the smaller unit and its position may be reviewed in a discussion of the parent corporation. Look at Chapter 4 for a description of your options for access to brokerage reports.

Use investment advisory publications for information about:

- Financial Data
- Company Strategies
- Industry Outlook

PERIODICAL AND NEWSPAPER ARTICLES

Articles in periodicals and newspapers may prove to be the most valuable source of information for a subsidiary or division. Many corporate units are well known in their own right, and industry watchers and investors are interested in their achievements. Because of this, articles that report solely on an individual business segment or unit within a corporation are frequently published. In addition, articles about the parent corporation may include significant comments about the subsidiary or division.

A number of conditions enhance the likelihood of finding an article about a subsidiary in a major national publication. For example, is the parent company well known nationally? Does the subsidiary have its own national reputation? Is it the producer of a familiar consumer product or service? Has it recently experienced a notable event—an anniversary, a new product introduction, a reorganization, or a merger or buyout—that would draw outside attention? Is it involved in a cutting-edge industry, a highly volatile one, or one facing a challenge from government regulation or foreign competition? Any of these factors will raise interest in a company and increase the possibility of an article being written about it, its parent corporation, or its industry.

The periodical and newspaper indexes commonly used for company research of any kind are the same ones to consult for articles about a subsidiary or division. Remember, duplication will be present in these indexes, but each may also list some unique articles. The most familiar and widely available business indexes are these:

Business Periodicals Index. H. W. Wilson Co. Monthly.

As the best-known business index, *BPI* is likely to be available in all but the smallest libraries. Begin looking for articles by checking under the subsidiary name. Try also the parent company name and the industry for articles with a broader perspective.

Predicasts F&S Index United States. Predicasts, Inc. Weekly.

With its emphasis on companies and products, this may be the best index for quickly discovering articles on the individual units of a company. *F&S*'s coverage of trade journals adds to its research value. In addition to the familiar paper copies, *F&S* and *BPI* may also be available in your library as online databases or compact disc products.

Business Index. Information Access Co. Monthly.

ABI/Inform. University Microforms Inc. Bimonthly.

The number of periodicals covered by these two indexes make them very valuable when searching for less well-known companies. Libraries, however, may not carry all the periodicals that they index. Neither of these indexes is available in paper. *Business Index* will be found as microfilm or a compact disc; *ABI/Inform* as an online database or compact disc.

The Wall Street Journal Index. University Microforms Inc. Monthly.

The best-known daily business newspaper in the United States, *The Wall Street Journal* has coverage of all kinds of companies across the nation. The "Corporate News" section lists articles under company name; try both the subsidiary and the parent company names. Since the listings for large companies can be several columns long, read them carefully for mention of the subsidiary you are researching.

These indexes cover major national publications and trade journals with wide readership, but specialized trade journals and regional business periodicals with limited circulation may also carry articles about the subsidiary or division you are researching. Unfortunately, there is no easy way to locate articles in such publications. You can narrow the possibilities by identifying the major trade journals in a field and determining if and where they might be indexed. Use one of the periodical directories listed in Chapter 4 under "Periodical and Newspaper Articles" for this purpose. If the trade journals are not indexed, your alternative is to scan the table of contents of each issue for relevant articles. You may face similar problems using regional business publications. Although they cover local businesses more thoroughly, simply because of proximity and interest, they also are not widely indexed or available in libraries.

Don't overlook the local newspaper where a subsidiary is headquartered. Even if national interest in the company is minimal, on its own turf it may be big news, particularly if the company has a high profile and is a major employer. Newspapers from larger cities often have published indexes and newspaper indexes are increasingly available as online databases. Sometimes the full text of the newspaper is included online.

Online databases may, in fact, provide a useful alternative if you are unable to locate information in easily accessible

Use periodical and newspaper articles for information about:

- Facilities
- Company Size
- Product/Service
- Financial Data
- Company History
- Company Strategies
- Response to Difficulty
- Management/Employee Data
- Executive Biography
- Employee Morale
- Salaries
- Industry Outlook

sources. Some databases cover highly specialized materials, including regional and trade publications. A fee is usually charged to search these online indexes for information and to retrieve the articles. Learn more about electronic information possibilities in Chapter 12.

BIOGRAPHICAL SOURCES FOR TOP EXECUTIVES

The top executive of a subsidiary or division is usually named in the business directories mentioned earlier. If the subsidiary has its own separate listing in a directory, additional officers may be named. Finding biographical details about these individuals may be difficult, however. The biographical directories described in Chapter 4 rarely include any but the most senior management. Check those, however, before going on to other options.

If the well-known directories from Chapter 4 do not include the individuals you seek and this information is important to your evaluation of a company, try these suggestions. First, carefully review the periodical articles you have gathered. They may include biographical data about the top managers of the subsidiary. The articles may, at a minimum, give a sense of the attitudes and character of top management. Ask at your library for a current local or regional biographical directory for the area where the company is located. With its more limited scope, such a directory may include the executives you seek. Check the major newspaper where the company is located. While the company may be overlooked nationally, on the local scene it and its executives may make news.

Be prepared to look beyond the library. If you have contacts within the company, ask them about the top executives. Don't forget that their comments, however revealing and helpful, will be colored by their own experience and will include some hearsay and gossip. The business editor of the newspaper in the subsidiary's location may be familiar with the top executives of the company and willing to share information and insight. Remember that your primary interest is in the executives' training and career, but civic and avocational activities can also be revealing.

COMPANY HISTORY, PRODUCTS AND SERVICES, AND INDUSTRY ANALYSES

The availability of published information sources for subsidiaries and divisions in these three categories may be limited. The best option for finding such information in the library may be a periodical or newspaper article. Of the information sources reviewed for these factors for public corporations in Chapter 4, several concentrate solely on the dominant partner in the corporation. However, possibilities exist for the subsidiary also.

If a subsidiary had an independent existence before becoming a part of another corporation, it may have its own company history. Check for a copy in your library, keeping in mind that such a history will be dated and deal only with events before the present merger or takeover. Read the periodical articles you have collected for company history. Significant facts may be included in a discussion of the company as it is today. It is more important to be acquainted with the history of the parent company that now controls the subsidiary. Review the suggestions for locating company history in the preceding chapter and concentrate on understanding the parent's background.

You can research products or services of a subsidiary in the same way as those of a parent corporation. Published resources make little, if any, distinction between company types in describing products. A parent company's annual report may include a discussion of a subsidiary's products or services, particularly if they make a notable contribution to the corporation's success and total revenues. Review periodical articles for product data also. Techniques suggested for evaluating products outside the library in Chapter 4 will also be effective for the product of a subsidiary, but decide how important this information is to your evaluation and budget research time accordingly.

Many corporations concentrate their products and services within a single industry category or several closely related ones. In such cases, studying the industry of the parent company will provide adequate insight into the current industry outlook for a subsidiary or division. However, it is not unusual for a corporation to have interests in several divergent industries. In this case, review the industry of the unit you are researching and also become familiar with its parent's primary industry. Look back at the information sources suggested in Chapter 4 for researching industries. They will be equally useful in surveying the industry of a subsidiary or division.

Use industry analyses for information about:

- Company Size
- Product/Service
- Financial Data
- Industry Outlook

Personal contacts and sources outside the library may also reveal some aspects of subsidiaries or divisions that are not easily found in published resources. Chapters 7 and 8 will provide direction for that kind of research—read them if you need ideas.

Use sources outside the library for information about:

- Facilities
- Financial Data
- Company Strategies
- Response to Difficulty
- Management/Employee Data
- Executive Biography
- Employee Morale
- Salaries
- Industry Outlook

A final suggestion for researching a subsidiary or division: Spend time studying the parent as well as its "junior." The parent sets the corporate management priorities and style. Decisions about expansion, increased spending, annual wage increases, advertising budgets—in fact, anything financial in nature—will probably be made at the top corporate level and will depend on the overall financial health of the corporation. Scan all of Chapter 4 on publicly owned parent companies and follow up on useful suggestions there. Be aware, too, of the parent's other subsidiaries and how they are functioning. It is not necessary to study them in depth, but you should know if any of them are encountering major difficulties that may affect the entire corporation, including the unit you are researching.

6 Researching Foreign-Owned Corporations

As foreign business competition has grown and the number of foreign-owned companies in the U.S. has increased, American interest in international firms has also flourished. With new investment opportunities in the European Community, economic change in Eastern Europe, and free trade agreements with Canada and Mexico sustaining American interest in foreign business operations, a corresponding growth in international business information sources has taken place. This development may make research into foreign-owned companies somewhat easier for you.

Foreign-owned firms, however, are not generally subject to U.S. financial disclosure laws. Because financial data are difficult to obtain, other information may also be hard to locate. Most libraries have limited collections of foreign and international materials and you may need to spend more time to find the necessary facts for evaluating a foreign-owned company as an employer. In addition, searching for data on a foreign-owned company means researching two companies: first, the American firm that is, in fact, the U.S. subsidiary or division of a foreign company and, second, the parent foreign corporation. Nevertheless, several research options should be readily available (see Figure 6.1).

Look for ***Location*** in
- Directories

Look for ***Facilities*** in
- Directories
- Credit Reports
- Articles
- Personal Contacts

Look for ***Company Size*** in
- Directories
- Credit Reports
- Articles
- Business Rankings

Look for ***Product/Service*** in
- Directories
- Credit Reports
- Articles
- Industry Surveys

Look for ***Financial Data*** in
- Credit Reports
- Brokerage Reports
- Articles
- Industry Averages
- Personal Contacts

Look for ***Company History*** in
- Articles
- Published Histories

Look for ***Company Strategies*** in
- Articles
- Personal Contacts

Look for ***Response to Difficulty*** in
- Articles
- Personal Contacts

Look for ***Management/Employee Data*** in
- Articles
- Personal Contacts

Look for ***Executive Biography*** in
- Directories
- Articles
- Personal Contacts

Look for ***Employee Morale*** in
- Articles
- Personal Contacts

Look for ***Salaries*** in
- Books
- Periodicals/Newspapers
- Employment Offices
- Personal Contacts

Look for ***Industry Outlook*** in
- Articles
- Industry Surveys
- Trade Associations
- Personal Contacts

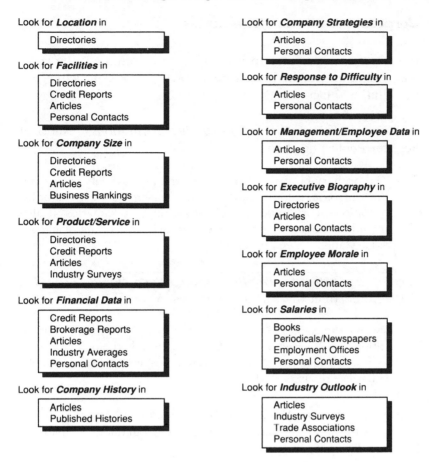

Figure 6.1 Research checklist for a foreign-owned company.

DIRECTORIES

Always a good starting point, a directory usually contains the headquarters location, the top executives, major product lines, and often the total number of employees and approximate annual sales of a firm—all in one source. Depending on the purpose and scope of the directory, it may include other information. Foreign-owned companies will appear in several types of directories, each offering similar but sometimes unique items of information.

Corporate Affiliation Directories

In Chapter 3, these directories helped to determine if the company being investigated was foreign-owned. Look at them again for additional facts:

International Directory of Corporate Affiliations. National Register Publishing. Annual.

> The primary purpose of this directory, also available as an online database, is to establish the relationship between major international corporations and their foreign subsidiaries. It also includes a selection of basic facts about both the American subsidiary and its foreign parent.

America's Corporate Families and International Affiliates. Dun & Bradstreet Information Services. Annual.

> Twelve thousand U.S. subsidiaries of over 3,000 foreign corporations are covered here, with information on the parent as well as the subsidiary. U.S. parent companies and their foreign subsidiaries are also listed.

Jeffrey S. Arpan and David A. Ricks. *Directory of Foreign Manufacturers in the United States,* 4th ed. Georgia State University Business Press. 1990.

> Use this directory if researching a manufacturer. The information included is very brief—name and address of the U.S. enterprise, its product, the foreign parent's name and headquarters country.

Directory of Foreign Investment in the U.S. Gale Research Inc. 1991.

> This directory has a business section covering 10,000 companies in all business lines. All have 10 percent or more foreign ownership. Standard directory information is provided for each U.S. firm, along with the name and address of the foreign owner.

While none of these directories can provide all you want to know about a foreign-owned company, all provide basic facts in quick, simple fashion.

National and International Business Directories

The national business directories recommended for basic facts about leading U.S. corporations and their subsidiaries are also useful for U.S. subsidiaries of foreign firms. They include the *Million Dollar Directory* (Dun & Bradstreet Information Services, annual), *Standard and Poor's Register of Corporations, Directors, and Executives* (Standard & Poor's Corp., annual), *Thomas Register of American Manufacturers* (Thomas Publishing Co., annual), and *Ward's Business Directory of U.S. Private and Public Companies* (Gale Research Inc., annual). Chapter 4 outlines the content of all these directories. As the usual criterion for inclusion in these directories is size, not nationality of ownership, a foreign-owned U.S. firm would not be excluded. Expect to find such firms listed if their size or national reputation qualifies them. Foreign ownership is not always indicated.

For basic information about the foreign parent of a U.S. subsidiary, consult a foreign or an international business directory. Few libraries will have an extensive collection of these, for they are often expensive and little used in comparison with U.S. directories. Business publisher Dun & Bradstreet offers a variety of directories for Canada, Europe, Latin America, and the Far East; European publishers also provide directories for several countries. Ask for those available at your library. An international directory found in many libraries is:

Principal International Businesses. Dun & Bradstreet Information Services. Annual.

> With listings for 50,000 companies in 140 countries, this directory covers most of the top companies of the world. Although the information provided is brief, it includes address, telephone, lines of business, top executive, number of employees,

sales, and founding date. If a company is a subsidiary, its parent is noted (see Figure 6.2).

A number of international and foreign business directories are available as online databases. The cost of searching these databases can be substantial, particularly if you retrieve all the information available for a company. However, if data about the foreign parent is important to your evaluation of a prospective employer and no other sources are available, this may be a good option. Ask about availability and the approximate cost of searching such a database.

Specialized Directories

Don't overlook specialized directories devoted to a single industry or geographic region as a source of additional information about American subsidiaries of foreign corporations. Although

ARGENTINA

)0-2796 IMP EXP
BORATORIOS SA
'ETH INTERNATIONAL LTD
IE PRODUCTS CORP, WAYNE,
\TES)
, Quilmes, Bs As 1003
5OWYETHIL
Employees 397
41
'rep
Presidente

)0-4107 IMP EXP
NSON DE ARGENTINASACI
HNSON & JOHNSON, NEW
J, UNITED STATES)
os Aires 1414
Employees 467
37

D-U-N-S 97-000-3281 IMP EXP
GREEN INDUSTRIAS REFRACTARIAS ARGENTINAS A P SA
(*Subsidiary of* A P GREEN REFRACTORIES CO, MEXICO, MO, UNITED STATES)
L N Alem 639, Buenos Aires 1001
Cable/Telex 23369GREENAR
Sales 4 091 M *Employees* 180
Year Started 1935
SIC 3255 5085
Clay Refractories
Dr Juan Bernardo Etchegoin H, *Presidente*

D-U-N-S 97-000-0295 IMP EXP
GREFAR SAIC
(*Subsidiary of* INDUSTRIAS PENOLES SA DE CV, MEXICO, DF, MEXICO)
L N Alem 986, Buenos Aires 1001
Cable/Telex 24208GREFAR
Sales 16 504 M *Employees* 238
Year Started 1961

Figure 6.2 Typical entries, *Principal International Businesses.* Copyright © 1992 Dun & Bradstreet Inc. All rights reserved. Reprinted by permission.

some directories provide detailed descriptions, others contain only addresses. Check for those available in your library. State industrial directories are another possibility. If the foreign-owned firm is a manufacturer, the state directory may add new facts. For more information on specialized directories, see that section of Chapter 4.

Use directories for information about:

- Location
- Facilities
- Company Size
- Product/Service
- Executive Biography

FINANCIAL REPORTS AND STATEMENTS

Financial information for a foreign-owned company may be difficult to locate primarily because documents for the foreign parent may not be readily available. Financial disclosure rules vary from country to country, but generally, foreign corporate regulations are less stringent than those of the United States. Furthermore, if copies of the foreign corporation's financial documents are available, they may be in the language of the company's headquarters location.

You are researching one unit of the corporation, the American-based subsidiary. Since foreign financial regulations are less demanding than those of the United States, the contribution of an American subsidiary to a foreign corporation's fiscal performance may be difficult, perhaps even impossible, to ascertain. Segment data may not be available. If it is, the U.S. firm is likely to be grouped together with other subsidiaries or divisions of the corporation. Only if the firm is the sole company in a specific segment or country, may it be possible to determine its proportionate role in the corporation's overall success. If the firm is a subsidiary of a privately owned foreign company, chances of discovering financial details are extremely slim.

Financial Documents

What financial data are readily available for foreign corporations? Although U.S. investor interest in foreign corporations has grown in recent years and with it a demand for corporate financial documents from abroad, access to original financial documents is limited. Few libraries have them. Copies of documents for some foreign corporations are available for purchase through a U.S. document delivery firm, Disclosure, Inc. Call or write to them directly for information about availability and cost (Disclosure, Inc., 5161 River Road, Bethesda MD 20816, 800-638-8241).

Comprehensive Financial Services

In lieu of official financial documents for foreign corporations, alternative sources such as the following may answer some questions:

Moody's International Manual. Moody's Investors Service. Annual with updates.

> One of a series of volumes that report on publicly owned firms in a variety of business areas, this publication focuses on major foreign corporations in over 100 countries. The information for each of the 5,000 companies covered usually includes a brief corporate history, including mergers, name changes, and the founding date. Next are listed business lines and products, plants and properties, and the subsidiaries of the corporation. A three-to-five-year summary financial statement, including balance sheet statistics, follows. The current status of the company's stocks is also outlined. Data here refer to the entire corporation; no segment information is given.

Worldscope Company Profiles. Gale Research Inc. Annual.

> This publication analyzes individual companies and industries abroad, surveying 6,500 companies in the United States and 23 other countries. Data for each company includes income statement and balance sheet, financial and investment ratios, stock

data, and company accounting practices. Individual segment detail is not provided.

Global Company Handbook. CIFAR. 1991.

The financial performance of 7,500 of the world's leading companies from 48 countries are outlined here. Five years of financial variables, industry and country averages, and several rankings highlight comparative performance nationally, regionally, and worldwide.

Directory of Multinationals, 4th ed. Stockton Press. 1992.

This set covers 450 of the world's leading multinational corporations. Along with standard directory information, it provides five years of financial data with some geographic breakdown. Profits, sales, debt, assets, capital expenditure, and R&D expenditure may be included in the data provided for each corporation.

The first three of these sources may also be available in your library in electronic format, either as online databases or compact disc products.

U.S. Financial Disclosure Reports

A few hundred of the world's largest publicly owned foreign firms trade their stock on U.S. stock exchanges. Most, but not all, of them have American subsidiaries. Because their stocks are traded on U.S. exchanges, these foreign corporations are subject to the financial disclosure regulations of the U.S. Securities and Exchange Commission. They file an annual report with the SEC—a 20-F form—similar in content to the 10-K form filed by U.S. public companies. Chapter 4 provides a full description of the data required in the 10-K form. If your library has a collection of 10-K reports, the 20-F filings may be included with them. Request copies of the latest 20-F annual filings directly from the SEC or the commercial report service, Disclosure, Inc., mentioned earlier in this chapter and in Chapter 4. But, remember, this is a report on the entire corporation, not just the American subsidiary. Information will be supplied for the corporation's various business segments as required, but not for each individual subsidiary or plant location in the United States.

Use financial reports and statements for information about:

- Facilities
- Product/Service
- Company Size
- Financial Data

INVESTMENT ADVISORY PUBLICATIONS

Although the purpose of advisory publications is to provide background data and analysis for the investor, the commentary can also provide information useful in evaluating a company as a prospective employer.

Advisory Services

The best-known investment services, with few exceptions, discuss investment opportunities in American-owned public firms. The chief exceptions are foreign firms traded on U.S. stock exchanges. If the parent corporation of the American subsidiary you are evaluating is one of these, look at one or all of these publications:

Value Line Investment Survey. Value Line, Inc. Weekly.

> This advisory service is widely available. About 50 Canadian, European, and Japanese companies traded on U.S. exchanges are analyzed on a rotating quarterly basis. Note especially the narrative section, which analyzes a company's current position and its short-term outlook. A subsidiary's activities are often highlighted.

Standard Stock Reports. Standard & Poor's Corp. Quarterly.

Moody's Handbook of Common Stocks. Moody's Investors Service. Quarterly.

> The comments and the financial summaries in these two investor services focus on the total corporate unit. If the foreign

parent of an American firm is included, the information can provide a survey of the general outlook for the corporation as well as clues about the climate for its growth and expansion in the United States.

Brokerage Reports

Brokerage reports provide a second type of investment advice. Analysts at investment banks and research firms around the world study firms and industries and prepare in-house reports. These reports, based on expert knowledge and familiarity with current trends, have wide application for the evaluation of companies and may discuss subsidiaries as well as the parent corporation in some detail. The published reports are seldom available in libraries but you may request copies directly from a brokerage if you can identify the ones you want.

Alternatively, you can gain access to them electronically. For example, the compact disc service and online database *Investext* (Thomson Financial Networks, weekly updates) provides reports of about 125 investment firms worldwide. *ICC International Business Research* (ICC Stockbroker Research, Ltd. and Key Note Ltd., weekly updates), another online database, has brokerage reports for British and European companies. The documents covered by these electronic services may not discuss an American subsidiary in any detail. Also, since this form of access can be a costly option, examine your other information possibilities first.

A final possibility: Check whether the American firm you are researching or its industry is reviewed in *The Wall Street Transcript* (The Wall Street Transcript Corporation, weekly). The discussions between industry analysts and brokers found here cover many types of companies and can illuminate a number of issues about financial performance. Chapter 4 provides more information about this publication.

Use investment advisory publications for information about:

- Financial Data

PERIODICAL AND NEWSPAPER ARTICLES

Businesses are increasingly global in their outlook and you will find a corresponding increase in coverage of foreign firms, international competition, and worldwide trade in many periodicals and newspapers. Look for articles that feature the subsidiary alone, its parent, or the corporation as an integrated multinational firm. Articles may, in fact, be your best source of information about an American subsidiary. If it is a subsidiary of a privately owned or small foreign firm, articles may be your *only* source of information.

How difficult will it be to find articles? If a company was independent or American owned in the past, reader interest may continue, particularly if the American unit has a national reputation or is a leader in its industry. Other firms will arouse interest if they are the first venture of a major foreign firm in the United States or the first foreign-owned firm in a particular locality. Although some foreign firms are unfamiliar or uncomfortable with the American tradition of open information access, most American managers are aware of the value and necessity of furnishing information to the media through appropriate channels.

Articles potentially provide a wide variety of information. Look at them for clues to management strategy, financial status, organizational structure, marketing plans, employee relations, executive biography, new products, and much more. Use this information to supplement whatever you find in other sources and to bring it up to date.

Scan the suggestions in Chapters 4 and 5 about the types of periodicals to examine. The same indexes useful for locating articles about U.S. public corporations and their subsidiaries are also good sources for articles on a foreign-owned subsidiary: *Business Periodicals Index* (H. W. Wilson Co., monthly), *Predicasts F&S Index United States* (Predicasts, Inc., weekly), *Business Index* (Information Access Co., monthly), and *ABI/Inform* (University Microforms, Inc., monthly). Search for both the American subsidiary and its foreign parent in the indexes. In addition, look for recent survey articles on economic conditions in the parent company's home nation. You need not become an expert in international finance, for your goal is to evaluate the American-based subsidiary as a prospective employer. Awareness of major economic changes in the company's home country, however, may help you judge the climate for long-term investment and strategic plans within the corporation.

For periodical and newspaper indexes with interest or focus on foreign and international companies, look also for these specialized indexes in your library:

Predicasts F&S Index Europe. Predicasts Inc. Monthly.

Predicasts F&S Index International. Predicasts Inc. Monthly.

These are companion indexes to the *Predicasts F&S Index U.S.* and may also be available in some libraries as a compact disc or an online database. They provide the same convenient access to current articles on companies, products, and industries in Europe and throughout the rest of the world. Divided into two sections (Part One arranged by industry and product and Part Two by company name), they also index a wide selection of business and industry publications. One drawback to these indexes is access to the specialized periodicals they cover.

Index to the Financial Times. Research Publications Ltd. Monthly.

The Times Index. Research Publications Ltd. Monthly.

The *Financial Times* is a highly respected daily business newspaper originating in Britain, easily recognized by the pink paper it is printed on. Somewhat equivalent to *The Wall Street Journal,* its scope is international with emphasis on Britain and Europe. The *Times* of London is Britain's most venerable and authoritative newspaper. Its business section covers British and European companies as well as many international firms. Using either of these newspapers gives you the advantage of English language coverage, with a non-U.S. perspective on a foreign company and its activities. Look for the newspapers and their indexes in larger libraries. The *Financial Times* is also available as a full-text online database.

Use periodical and newspaper articles for information about:

- Facilities
- Company Size
- Product/Service
- Financial Data
- Company History
- Company Strategies
- Response to Difficulty
- Management/Employee Data
- Executive Biography
- Employee Morale
- Salaries
- Industry Outlook

BIOGRAPHICAL SOURCES FOR TOP EXECUTIVES

Information about the background and training of executives in a foreign-owned company is of interest for two reasons: It can help you understand the experience and skills valued in top management and it may suggest certain aspects of your own career to highlight in your resume.

Split your research into two parts again—the American firm and its foreign parent. The name of the president or chief executive officer of either company may be easy to identify, but biographical details are harder to discover. Identifying additional individuals as you move down the management ladder becomes more difficult and biographical details more scarce, even for the American subsidiary. For chief executives of the U.S. firm, check the biographical sources suggested in Chapter 4. They should be your first stop. You may also learn additional facts from company profiles in periodical and newspaper articles. However, the best option may be a contact within the company, if you have one.

What about the executives of the foreign parent? Be prepared to become an amateur detective if you want to learn details. There is no widely available directory of international business executives and, but for a few flamboyant exceptions, many of these individuals shun publicity. In fact, you may not need to know much about foreign corporate executives to evaluate a company as an employer. You may want to know their names—the directories listed in the first section of this chapter should list them. You may want to know the tempo or mood the executives set for the company, but you are most likely to discover that in a periodical article. If you are determined to find additional biographical information, begin with a national biographical directory for the country where the firm is headquartered. Although a biographical directory is published for almost every country, most U.S. libraries have only a few of these. Ask to see whatever is available for the country you are interested in.

COMPANY HISTORY

Company history provides an appreciation for the traditions that pervade a company and an understanding of the events that brought it to its present position. A few details of a company's past may be in sources previously mentioned. Periodical articles, financial reports, and directories may all include a brief summary of the establishment and early years of a firm. If you kept notes of these facts as you found them, you may already have an outline history. Consider now some sources of further information. Remember you are looking at two companies—the U.S. subsidiary and its foreign parent.

If a book has been written about a company, it may be available in your library, listed in the catalog under the company name as a subject. Look for the names of both companies: American subsidiary and foreign parent. If nothing is available, look for a history of its industry. The content of any book will be somewhat dated but don't worry—you are seeking a history, not yesterday's stock prices. Scan for major events and prime movers and update this information with more recent periodical or newspaper articles.

Everybody's Business (Doubleday, 1990), the collection of company profiles suggested for thumbnail histories in Chapter 4, includes 35 of the largest foreign companies. See if your company is one of those included. Two similar volumes profiling multinational companies are:

Milton Moskowitz. *The Global Marketplace: 102 of the Most Influential Companies Outside America.* Macmillan. 1987.

Each company included has a four- to five-page sketch briefly defining the firm's background and its current position. The profiles give a feeling for the tone of the company and a hint of the workplace atmosphere found there.

Philip Mattera. *World Class Business: a Guide to the 100 Most Powerful Global Corporations.* Henry Holt and Co. 1992.

Selected on the basis of size and international activity, the 100 companies profiled here are a microcosm of important and influential firms worldwide. Most foreign firms included have U.S. operations. Historical development, current operations, labor relations, and environmental record are outlined for each.

Another source of company history for very large corporations around the world is:

International Directory of Company Histories. St. James Press. 5 volumes. 1988–1992.

Twelve hundred of the world's largest and most influential companies are included in this set. Each has US$2 billion in sales or is a leader in its industry worldwide. Standard directory information is given for each firm, followed by a two- to three-page history. At the end of each history are suggestions for further reading—usually a full book on the company or its industry. The histories are grouped by industry categories so that you can compare the backgrounds of leading international competitors.

Additional suggestions that may help to locate a company history for the American subsidiary can be found in the appropriate sections of Chapters 4 and 5.

PRODUCT AND SERVICES INFORMATION

The techniques for researching the products or services of an American firm with foreign ownership are no different from those used to evaluate the products of an American-owned firm. Periodical and newspaper articles may again prove to be the most valuable source of easily accessible information.

Brands and Their Companies (Gale Research Inc., Annual), described in Chapter 4, will assist in determining the brand names of products manufactured, imported, or distributed by American firms. A companion publication *International Brands and Their Companies* (Gale Research Inc., 2nd ed. 1990) surveys products manufactured by firms outside the U.S. For strategies to use in evaluating the products, consult the appropriate section of Chapter 4. Read the suggestions and follow up on those that are applicable to your product or company.

INDUSTRY ANALYSES

Knowledge of the industry in which a company competes is a fundamental aspect of preparing to evaluate an employer. You must understand the arena the company competes in, the challenges it faces from external forces, and the outlook for its segment of the national economy. Of primary importance is the company in its American setting, functioning and competing within the American economy. However, you also want to be aware of the international arena in which a company competes.

For library resources to help evaluate the American aspects of your industry, read the relevant section of Chapter 4. Of particular value for an overview will be:

Standard and Poor's Industry Surveys. Standard & Poor's Corp. Annual with quarterly updates.

U.S. Industrial Outlook. U.S. Department of Commerce. Annual.

> Read the surveys contained in those two publications primarily for their assessment of the outlook for various industries in the United States. However, both also include consideration of foreign competition and global economic outlook where relevant.

Don't overlook the additional perspective that periodical and newspaper articles may provide. Scan them for broad discussions of industry trends and for the outlook in the United States as well as internationally. Look again at the *Worldscope Country Profiles* and the *Global Company Handbook* mentioned in the section on financial information sources earlier in this chapter. In addition to profiles of leading international companies, these publications both contain comparative rankings, including worldwide company rankings within industries and by industry within a country.

The publications of Business International are another source of global economic and industry outlook data. This publisher provides a series of weekly newsletters surveying business conditions in major world regions. Individual countries are profiled on a rotating basis, three-year economic forecasts are regularly updated, and the corporate strategies of leading multinational corporations are analyzed. Although these publications are found only in very large libraries, they are also available as an online database.

Online databases that cover international corporate and economic news are, in fact, an additional option to explore in researching a company, especially the foreign parent. Databases derive their information from periodicals, newspapers, and newswire stories from many countries. However, the files are often expensive to search and you may have difficulty obtaining the documents cited in the search. Consider how important this information may be to your evaluation of a prospective employer, survey other available resources, and then decide if you need to use electronic sources. A librarian can advise you about database availability and approximate costs for a search.

Use industry analyses for information about:

- Company Size
- Product/Service
- Financial Data
- Industry Outlook

You may also want to consider information sources outside the library; Chapters 7 and 8 offer suggestions for exploring these possibilities. Don't overlook your personal contacts. They can also help you to better understand certain aspects of foreign-owned corporations. Options for the personal approach have been noted briefly throughout this chapter and are also covered in more detail in Chapters 7 and 8.

Use sources outside the library for information about:

- Facilities
- Financial Data
- Company Strategies
- Response to Difficulty
- Executive Biography
- Employee Morale
- Salaries
- Industry Outlook

Before researching a foreign-owned firm, you may want to review Chapter 4. Although it deals with publicly owned American corporations, many of the suggestions found there will be helpful for all types of companies.

7 Researching Privately Held Corporations

A privately held company presents a number of challenges to anyone seeking information to evaluate it as a prospective employer. Its financial status is not routinely revealed like that of a publicly owned company. Most private companies are also reluctant to disclose other aspects of their activities. Because information is difficult to obtain, private companies may be only infrequently or superficially reported on in the business press. However, don't equate a preference for discretion with a failure to succeed. Many of America's largest and best-known firms are privately held; for example, Hallmark Cards, Levi Strauss, U.S. Sprint, or Domino's Pizza.

This chapter considers information sources only for the largest privately held corporations: those with national prominence in their industry or significant financial assets or sales (see Figure 7.1). Because there is considerable public interest in these companies, particularly those with consumer products and services, they are listed and analyzed in a number of publications.

DIRECTORIES

A directory may be the most accessible source of information about a privately held company. Location, top executive,

Look for ***Location*** in

- Directories

Look for ***Facilities*** in

- Directories
- Credit Reports
- Articles
- Government Offices
- Personal Contacts

Look for ***Company Size*** in

- Directories
- Credit Reports
- Articles
- Business Rankings
- Government Offices

Look for ***Product/Service*** in

- Directories
- Credit Reports
- Articles
- Industry Surveys

Look for ***Financial Data*** in

- Credit Reports
- Brokerage Reports
- Articles
- Industry Averages
- Government Offices
- Personal Contacts

Look for ***Company History*** in

- Articles
- Published Histories

Look for ***Company Strategies*** in

- Articles
- Personal Contacts

Look for ***Response to Difficulty*** in

- Articles
- Government Offices
- Personal Contacts

Look for ***Management/Employee Data*** in

- Articles
- Personal Contacts

Look for ***Executive Biography*** in

- Directories
- Articles
- Personal Contacts

Look for ***Employee Morale*** in

- Articles
- Personal Contacts

Look for ***Salaries*** in

- Books
- Periodicals/Newspapers
- Employment Offices
- Personal Contacts

Look for ***Industry Outlook*** in

- Articles
- Industry Surveys
- Trade Associations
- Personal Contacts

Figure 7.1 Research checklist for a large, private company.

products, number of employees, and approximate annual sales are commonly found here. Make careful note of all the facts presented in a directory. It may be difficult to find additional information on a private company elsewhere, and the information also may provide valuable clues to other sources. Look again at the directories in Chapter 3 that helped to identify private companies.

Directory of Leading Private Companies. National Register Publishing Co. Annual.

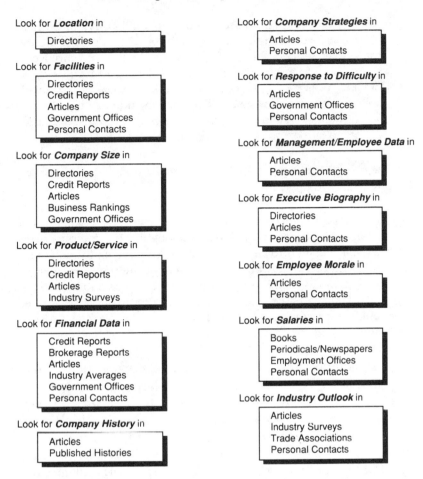

About 7,000 companies are listed in this directory; all of them have sales over $10 million. Included for each company are the following: address, lines of business, number of employees, state where incorporated, number of plants and facilities, and outside service firms (accountant, bank, insurer). Where available, financial data is given. This may include estimated sales, assets, liabilities, and net worth. Any wholly owned subsidiaries of the private companies are also briefly profiled.

Ward's Business Directory of U.S. Private and Public Companies. Gale Research Inc. Annual.

Since this directory has no minimum size criteria, companies of all sizes and types are included. Among the 100,000 plus firms listed are many private companies, both large and small. Standard directory information is given, including annual sales where available. One volume of the set contains a ranked list of the 1,000 largest private companies in the directory as well as rankings of companies by industry. Use this for comparisons among major firms (see Figure 7.2).

In addition to these two directories, other national business directories also include many of the largest private companies. The best known of these are the *Million Dollar Directory* (Dun & Bradstreet Information Services, annual), *Standard & Poor's Register of Corporations, Directors, and Executives* (Standard & Poor's Corp., annual), and *Thomas Register of American Manufacturers* (Thomas Publishing Co., annual). All are described in the directory section of Chapter 4. Usually the same data are given for private companies as for public, with the exception of financial data. Should you identify a company as a subsidiary of a privately held firm, look at the directories suggested in Chapter 5 for that form of incorporated unit. They may also contain facts not easily located elsewhere.

Note the suggestions for using specialized directories outlined in Chapter 4. Research on a privately held company will be based, in large part, on finding scattered facts and putting them together to form a full picture. The specialized directories, which often have data too particular for general interest, are sometimes a source of unexpected facts. State industrial directories are also a first-rate source for manufacturers, especially for local plants and facilities.

Astral Precision Equipment Co.
800 Busse Rd (708)439-1650
Elk Grove Village, IL 60007
Sales: $2.0 million **FY End:** 6-30
Employees: 15 **Type:** Private
SIC(s): 5084 Industrial Machinery & Equip
Description: Wholesale General industrial equipment
Officer(s): Xavier F. Kaufmann, *President*

Astrex Inc.
205 Express St (516)433-1700
Plainview, NY 11803
Sales: $20.0 million **FY End:** 3-31
Employees: 96 **Type:** Public
Ticker Symbol: ASI **Exchange:** AMEX
Founded: 1960 **Import**
SIC(s): 5065 Electronic Parts & Equip
Officer(s): Ronald Kass, *CEO*. Carol Hustedt, *Dir of Mktg & Sales*

Astrex Inc. Progress Electronics Co.
205 Express St (516)433-1700
Plainview, NY 11803
Sales: $4.4 million **FY End:** 3-31
Employees: 50 **Type:** Division
Founded: 1965 **Export**
Immediate Parent: Astrex Inc.
SIC(s): 5065 Electronic Parts & Equip
Description: Wholesale Electronic parts and equipment
Officer(s): Ronald S. Kass, *President*

Astro Air Inc.
P.O. Box 1988 (903)586-3691
Jacksonville, TX 75766 **FAX:** (214)586-7355
Sales: $26.0 million
Employees: 200 **Type:** Private
Founded: 1971
SIC(s): 3585 Refrigeration & Heating Equip
Officer(s): Rex Dacus, *CEO*. Cora Lowthian, *Mktg Mgr.*

Figure 7.2 Typical entries, *Ward's Business Directory of U.S. Private and Public Companies* (Vols. 1 & 2), edited by Julie E. Towell. Copyright © 1992 by Gale Research Inc. Reprinted by permission of the publisher.

Investigate your library's electronic business information sources. Several online databases include directory information for privately owned companies. For example, the *American Business Directory* (American Business Information, quarterly updates) and *D&B—Dun's Market Identifiers* (Dun & Bradstreet Information Services, quarterly) databases both cover several million public and private companies in all product areas and provide a current address and brief sales data. Electronic information sources are discussed in more detail in Chapter 12.

Use directories for information about:

- Location
- Facilities
- Company Size
- Product/Services
- Executive Biography

FINANCIAL REPORTS AND STATEMENTS

Privately held companies do not trade their shares of stock publicly and are not listed on the stock exchanges. Therefore, they do not have to provide financial disclosure statements to the U.S. Securities and Exchange Commission and do not publicly release annual reports to stockholders. The many financial services and investment advisory publications that analyze corporate actions and provide expert commentary for publicly owned corporations do not cover privately held companies, as their stock is not available for purchase by outside investors. Thus, details of financial status, statements of management strategy, and the selection of supporting facts and data, all of which appear in financial disclosure reports, are unavailable. The alternatives for this information are limited and not all will be in your library. Here are some options.

For the financial data, look carefully at the directories suggested earlier. Most will contain an estimate of annual sales; some may include additional financial data. Use special features such as the ranked list of private companies in *Ward's Directory* to provide useful comparisons. Among electronic sources, the

American Business Directory database, a directory of both public and private companies mentioned earlier, often provides market share data for the companies it covers. Other databases may include additional financial data. Survey all your available sources, gathering facts wherever possible.

Business credit reports are another potential source of financial data for some privately held companies. Credit reports evaluate a business's creditworthiness for financial institutions and other organizations with legitimate need for such information. Since these reports are confidential, they will not be accessible in your library; however, online databases containing extracts from credit reports may be available. These are expensive databases—a single credit report may cost $25 to $100 or more to retrieve, should one be available. Look at your other options thoroughly; then decide whether the potential value of the credit information offsets the high cost.

Explore periodical and newspaper articles for financial data and analysis, although the financial information in articles may be incomplete and widely scattered. To pursue the financial aspects of a private company, be prepared to extend your research beyond library sources (see recommendations for that step in the final part of this chapter).

Use financial reports and statements for information about:

- Facilities
- Company Size
- Product/Service
- Financial Data

PERIODICAL AND NEWSPAPER ARTICLES

Privately held companies are often discreet—some might say secretive—about their activities. Since they do not publish or make available an annual report or financial disclosure statement and are not covered in investment advisory publications, how does news of their achievements or failures reach the business community and the general public? In fact, such news often travels in the same way as it does for publicly owned companies—through periodical and newspaper articles.

In the case of a publicly owned company, a journalist often obtains information directly from the company, through public documents, press releases, and interviews. For a privately held company that prefers to avoid publicity, a journalist must be more aggressive, seeking information through inside contacts, industry watchers, financial analysts, trade association representatives, and others who may have access to privileged information. Because such material is harder to come by and often difficult to verify, private companies may be written about less frequently and with less thorough scrutiny. Nevertheless, they will be the subject of occasional periodical articles—particularly if the company is a major force in its industry, has a national reputation, or produces a well-known consumer product.

Periodical and newspaper articles will supplement the financial data in directories. Rankings of top private companies such as those appearing annually in *Business Week, Forbes,* or *Inc.* provide estimates of a company's financial performance and its standing within its industry. Chief executive officers of private companies occasionally consent to interviews that can be very revealing about the company, its management style, and its strategic outlook. Periodical articles about the company may include biographical data about top managers', their background and training. New product developments, marketing strategy, advertising campaigns—all may be covered in trade publications. An article may even include allusions to the company's beginnings through its evolution to its present position.

Periodical and Newspaper Indexes

Articles may appear in major business magazines, in trade journals and regional publications, and in nationally distributed as well as local newspapers. The indexes for business periodicals and newspapers described in Chapter 4 will be the best place to begin searching for articles on a private company. These include the *Business Periodicals Index* (H. W. Wilson Co., monthly), *Predicasts F&S Index United States* (Predicasts, Inc., weekly), *Business Index* (Information Access Co., monthly), and *ABI/*

Inform (University Microforms, Inc., monthly). Go back to Chapter 4 and read the relevant section for a full description of the indexes and their special features.

Start by using the index that seems most likely to contain articles on the company you are evaluating. If only one or two articles appear in that index, try the others. All may contain some duplicate references, but each may also list unique items. If you locate nothing, look for more general articles about the company's industry or even the firms that are its chief competitors. Either type of article may mention the firm you are evaluating. Online databases, discussed in Chapter 12, are an additional source of citations to periodical and newspaper articles, often from highly specialized sources. Consider this option carefully; a database search may lead to exactly the facts you are seeking.

In using periodical and newspaper indexes, keep in mind that you may encounter difficulty gaining access to all the periodicals cited. Your library's periodical collection may be limited, particularly in coverage of trade journals or regional business publications. Other libraries in your community may have the needed items. Start your research well ahead of any deadlines and your own library may be able to obtain copies of any especially useful articles through an "interlibrary loan" service. You must allow 10 to 20 days for this service and generally pay a modest fee. For an additional charge, some libraries provide telefacsimile rush service.

Use periodical and newspaper articles for information about:

- Facilities
- Company Size
- Product/Service
- Financial Data
- Company History
- Company Strategies
- Response to Difficulty
- Management/Employee Data
- Executive Biography
- Employee Morale
- Salaries
- Industry Outlook

COMPANY HISTORY, PRODUCTS, AND EXECUTIVE BIOGRAPHY

When seeking a company history, there is little to distinguish between a public company and a large private corporation. Look at the suggestions in Chapter 4 for guidelines. The same is true of product information. Again, look at the appropriate section of Chapter 4 for possible research strategies. Access to biographical information for executives of large private firms falls into the same pattern as biographies of public corporation executives. The sources and strategies for biography in Chapter 4 are good starting points for this factor, too. And don't forget to scan the periodical and newspaper articles you have gathered for the details they can add in these areas.

INDUSTRY ANALYSES

Difficulties are inevitable in researching a private company, but a broad-based knowledge of the industry a company competes in may substitute for missing facts. Review industry data with that premise in mind. For example, a thriving industry suggests a group of companies with a growing market, a successful financial environment, and a promising outlook. Marked exceptions to that overall picture, whether a public or private firm, will generally be noted. If an industry is facing rising foreign competition, shrinking markets, increased regulation, or other difficulty, any company competing in that industry is likely to face those problems and its future will be marked by its response to those challenges. Two familiar sources of industry analysis are the *U.S. Industrial Outlook* (U.S. Dept. of Commerce, annual) and *Standard & Poor's Industry Surveys* (Standard & Poor's Corp., annual with quarterly updates). The content and special features of both are described in the industry section of Chapter 4.

The financial ratios or industry averages that provide benchmarks for a company's financial performance will have reduced value in comparing a private firm with its industry if you have been unable to obtain a detailed financial statement for the firm. If you have financial data, the best known and most widely available of the ratio sources—the *RMA Annual*

Statement Studies (Robert Morris Associates, annual) and *Industry Norms and Key Business Ratios* (Dun & Bradstreet Information Services, annual)—are described in the industry section of Chapter 4.

The published rankings of companies within industries are an easy means of judging where the average company stands in an industry, but you may not have enough information about a private firm to make useful comparisons. The ranking sources are also described in the industry section of Chapter 4.

The ratios and the rankings may be useful in making assumptions about the private company's financial status. Even without a full financial statement, you can estimate the financial characteristics of a private firm using your available figures and the published financial ratios. Obviously, you must make such assumptions, which are based on industrywide norms, with extreme caution. Few companies will approximate the norm and without a good number of actual figures, your estimates may be far from accurate. Carefully compare the information you gather in this way with whatever else you know about a company.

Finally, a trade association may be a potential source of industry information. Formed to promote and protect the interests of participants in an industry, the trade association collects and disseminates information. Although some serve only their members, other associations are happy to assist anyone seeking information about their industry. Identify an appropriate association through the *Encyclopedia of Associations* (Gale Research Inc., annual), described in the industry section of Chapter 4, and call or write for information.

Use industry analyses for information about:

- Company Size
- Product/Service
- Financial Data
- Industry Outlook

INFORMATION SOURCES OUTSIDE THE LIBRARY

Because privately held companies are often reluctant to release information and are difficult for publishers and journalists to cover thoroughly, fewer information sources are available. You may need to extend your research, but be aware that considerable determination, as well as patience and many telephone calls or letters, may be needed to track down full information on private companies.

Begin by drawing up a list of the information you want but could not find in published resources, want to amplify further, or need to verify for accuracy. The key is determining who—a state agency, a local office, an individual—would have the answers to your questions. Think about each item and who would want or need to know those facts. Use your imagination, jot down the possibilities, and you have a list of potential contacts to pursue. The contacts will vary, depending on the company or industry you want to evaluate.

Chapter 8, on small, local companies, covers information interviews. Read it for tips on how to get good results from your contact calls. Don't forget that following through on your calls will take time. If you have started your research late and have an interview or need to respond to a job advertisement in a day or two, you may have to forgo this step.

State Government Agencies

State agencies are a good place to begin. All states require companies that are incorporated within their borders, whether publicly or privately owned, to file annual reports. Before you hurry to your telephone to call the pertinent state agency, however, you should also know that few of these reports are very helpful. About 80 percent of the states require no more than annual registration forms, asking only for name, address, and chief corporate officers. States that require more information may ask for assets, value of property, value of inventory, and so on. To find out about state corporate records, try this book:

Leonard Fuld. *Competitor Intelligence.* John Wiley & Sons. 1985.

> A step-by-step guide to corporate intelligence gathering by an experienced practitioner, this volume includes a guide to the content of state corporate filings around the nation.

Find out what is required in the state where a company is incorporated; then call or write the appropriate state office to ask how to obtain copies of the company's reports. The information on file with the state may be rather dated, and a request for copies may take several days or weeks to fill.

Other state offices may have documents dealing with environmental inspections, occupational health and safety reports, commercial loans, or consumer complaints about companies located within the state borders. The content and availability of these documents will vary widely from state to state. All are likely to contain rather dated material and all will take patience and time to obtain. The employees of state agencies are neither researchers nor librarians. To help them fill your requests quickly and accurately, be as specific as possible in your queries. If you must make your requests by telephone rather than in person, the process may be difficult and slow. Your local library can provide addresses and telephone numbers of state agencies across the nation.

Local Agencies

Local government agencies and offices may also be helpful, particularly if the private company you are researching plays a dominant role in the community. A good starting place for an investigation is the chamber of commerce in the city where the company is located. Although these offices are primarily promotional agencies, to fulfill that function they gather a great deal of information about existing local businesses. It is not unusual for a chamber of commerce to have pertinent facts about a company on file and for staff members to have personal knowledge of a company's background and reputation. Another possibility is a local industrial development board. This group is engaged in attracting new business to a community and, like the chamber, is well acquainted with companies that have recently located in their area. Local chambers and industrial development boards around the nation are listed with addresses and telephone numbers in *World Chamber of Commerce Directory* (World Chamber of Commerce Directory, annual).

Expert Contacts

Another option to explore is contacting an "expert." The expert's identity will depend on the company you are researching. One possibility is a journalist who has written a recent article on the company or its industry in either a general business publication or a trade journal. Alternatively, contact the business editor of the newspaper for the area where the corporation or its facility is located. This approach may be most successful if the firm is one of the chief employers or a dominant civic presence in the city in question.

You may identify an industry analyst while examining the firm's industry. That individual may be familiar with the major private companies in the industry as well as the publicly owned ones. Call the analyst and ask if he or she can provide any background or "inside" information about the company that could help to evaluate it as an employer. Don't overlook industry competitors as potential experts. If nothing else, staff at rival companies will have opinions and hearsay evidence about the privately held company they must contend with in the marketplace.

Trade Association Staff

Trade associations and their role in promoting industries and serving companies have already been mentioned. Companies of all types and sizes or their employees may be members of the association, attend association-sponsored conferences and seminars, and meet or speak with association staff on a frequent basis. Because of this, trade association staff may be well acquainted with the status of all companies in their industry, private as well as public, or can suggest someone who is. Contact the association offices and ask if someone can assist or advise you.

Although fewer published resources provide information on privately held companies and you must expend more time and effort for less return when researching them, you can discover a great deal. To the information that you find in the library, add whatever you can easily obtain from outside sources, and you may be able to construct a well-developed profile of a privately held employer.

Use sources outside the library for information about:

- Facilities
- Company Size
- Financial Data
- Company Strategies
- Response to Difficulty
- Management/Employee Data
- Executive Biography
- Employee Morale
- Salaries
- Industry Outlook

8 Researching Small Local or Regional Companies

A company that has no national reputation, achieves modest sales and assets, is privately owned, and markets its products or services primarily to a local or regional area presents difficulties for anyone who wants to learn more about it. Published, easily accessible information will not be available for a company fitting this description simply because you seek it. Information resources that are easily explored in libraries for other types of companies rarely include small firms. Researchers who have studied such companies may not have made their findings known. Because of the scarcity of published materials, you must use initiative to investigate alternative sources of information, to call or visit state and local agencies, and to develop a network of personal contacts. The suggestions in the following discussion rely on the assumption that the small firm you want to research is headquartered in your locality (see Figure 8.1).

INFORMATION SOURCES IN THE LIBRARY

You can explore several possibilities for information about small local companies. Although few library resources discuss small

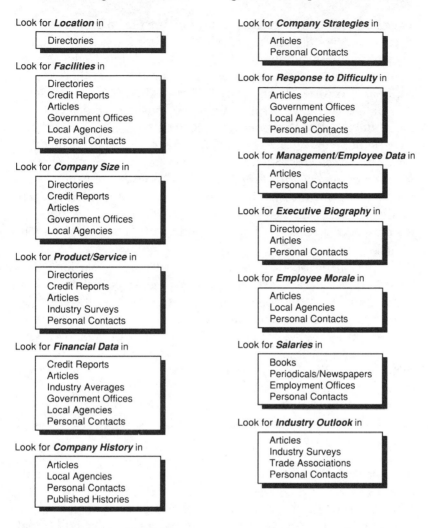

Look for ***Location*** in

- Directories

Look for ***Facilities*** in

- Directories
- Credit Reports
- Articles
- Government Offices
- Local Agencies
- Personal Contacts

Look for ***Company Size*** in

- Directories
- Credit Reports
- Articles
- Government Offices
- Local Agencies

Look for ***Product/Service*** in

- Directories
- Credit Reports
- Articles
- Industry Surveys
- Personal Contacts

Look for ***Financial Data*** in

- Credit Reports
- Articles
- Industry Averages
- Government Offices
- Local Agencies
- Personal Contacts

Look for ***Company History*** in

- Articles
- Local Agencies
- Personal Contacts
- Published Histories

Look for ***Company Strategies*** in

- Articles
- Personal Contacts

Look for ***Response to Difficulty*** in

- Articles
- Government Offices
- Local Agencies
- Personal Contacts

Look for ***Management/Employee Data*** in

- Articles
- Personal Contacts

Look for ***Executive Biography*** in

- Directories
- Articles
- Personal Contacts

Look for ***Employee Morale*** in

- Articles
- Local Agencies
- Personal Contacts

Look for ***Salaries*** in

- Books
- Periodicals/Newspapers
- Employment Offices
- Personal Contacts

Look for ***Industry Outlook*** in

- Articles
- Industry Surveys
- Trade Associations
- Personal Contacts

Figure 8.1 Research checklist for a small local or regional company.

companies, some key items are available. Start by looking at them and then explore options beyond the library.

Directories

A basic source of information for all other types of companies is a directory. General business directories with a national scope, as well as specialized directories for companies meeting certain criteria, are good starting points for determining a company's lines of business, number of employees, and annual sales. A few small companies with a local or regional market are included in national directories. Look at any of them—the company you seek may be listed. The best-known national business directories are the *Million Dollar Directory* (Dun & Bradstreet Information Services, annual), *Standard & Poor's Register of Corporations, Directors, and Executives* (Standard & Poor's Corp., annual), *Thomas Register of American Manufacturers* (Thomas Publishing Co., annual), and *Ward's Business Directory of U.S. Private and Public Companies* (Gale Research Inc., annual). All are described in the directory section of Chapter 4 and all of them will be widely available.

Specialized business directories that cover a particular industry or locality are also worth checking. They may include a fairly complete list of all companies that fit specific criteria, even small firms. Some directories, however, provide only names and addresses while others have valuable details about the companies listed. A guide to the many special business directories published on the national level is *Directories in Print* (Gale Research Inc., annual). See the directory section of Chapter 4 for a description of its features. Should this guide be unavailable, ask your reference librarian's assistance in locating relevant directories.

If the company is a manufacturer, check the state industrial directory. All 50 states have such directories, covering the manufacturers within their borders. Typically, they profile individual manufacturing locations in each state as well as managers, plant size, number of employees, products and a variety of additional details. Most state directories are restricted to manufacturers, but larger states may also have directories of nonmanufacturing firms. Check, too, for any additional local or regional directories available in your library.

Use directories for information about:

- Location
- Company Size
- Facilities
- Product/Service

Financial Sources

Financial information will be very difficult to obtain for small, local companies as virtually all of them will be privately held firms. Privately held corporations do not reveal details of their financial status, and small local companies are no exception. They do not publish annual stockholder reports or file financial disclosure statements. While estimates of the financial status of larger private companies may be available, you will rarely find estimates for small companies. Look closely at any published information, however, for there are always exceptions.

An alternative to consider is a credit-rating report. The reports, prepared by national financial services for businesses of all kinds, both large and small, are based on information supplied by banks, creditors, and public records. They are intended to inform a company's potential creditors about its financial stability. The reports are confidential and are sold only to financial organizations and to businesses and individuals with legitimate need for them. They are not available to the general public and as a result, you will not find them in libraries. However, excerpts from the reports are available in some libraries as online databases. Unfortunately, these are expensive databases so explore your other options fully before you proceed with a database search for a credit report.

Use financial sources for information about:

- Facilities
- Product/Service
- Company Size
- Financial Data

Periodical and Newspaper Articles

Even though a small company is unlikely to have been the subject of an article in the national press, its industry may have been studied. Trade magazines devoted to the industry and local and regional business journals may also be helpful in outlining current trends. Scan the periodical indexes suggested in Chapter

4 for relevant articles in general magazines or browse directly in specialized trade magazines and regional business journals. If a company issues its own newsletter, see if the local library has copies.

The newspaper for your locality and perhaps others from the surrounding area may be useful information sources, particularly if a company has a high profile in the community. News stories about the company's background and development, its top executives, current employment prospects, new products, or community activities are all possibilities. The challenge is to locate the issues that carried the stories, as most small newspapers are not indexed. Newspapers are increasingly available as online databases, making the retrieval of stories from some localities easier. Ask if the newspaper you want to scan is one of these. As an alternative to an index, many libraries clip and file stories from their local newspaper. If your library has a newspaper clipping file, it may include stories about local companies.

Use periodical and newspaper articles for information about:

- Facilities
- Company Size
- Product/Service
- Financial Data
- Company History
- Company Strategies
- Response to Difficulty
- Management/Employee Data
- Executive Biography
- Employee Morale
- Salaries
- Industry Outlook

Industry Analyses

Take full advantage of library materials dealing with a company's industry. No matter what its size, a company will be competing with others, large and small, facing similar economic conditions, employment trends, foreign competition, or government regulation. The more you know about the overall condition of the industry and the average performance and expectation of companies involved, the better you can judge the individual achievements and outlook of a company. A review of published resources for researching industries is found in Chapter 4. The *U.S. Industrial Outlook* (U.S. Dept. of Commerce, annual) or *Standard & Poor's Industry Surveys* (Standard & Poor's Corp., annual with quarterly updates), for example, are useful sources. Both provide current data and outlook analysis for a variety of industries and both are widely available in libraries.

Although financial data for a small company may be difficult to obtain, compare whatever you do find with the financial ratios for its industry. The industry section of Chapter 4 describes the best-known sources of financial ratios. An additional source of ratio analysis for use in evaluating smaller companies is:

Financial Studies of the Small Business. Financial Research Associates. Annual.

> Financial ratios and balance sheet/income statement data are provided for firms having a total capitalization under $250,000. Coverage is limited to 50 industries, primarily retail and service industries, but also a few manufacturers, wholesalers, and contractors.

Use industry analyses for information about:

- Product/Service
- Financial Data
- Industry Outlook

Trade Association Data

A potential source of industry information you should not overlook is the trade association that supports and promotes a company's industry. One of the usual responsibilities of a trade association is to inform the public about the activities, achievements, and challenges faced by companies participating in the industry. Most associations publish a newsletter or periodical, and many gather industrywide statistics. Although some associations serve only member companies, others provide information freely to all. Check the *Encyclopedia of Associations,* described in the industry section of Chapter 4, for a trade association relevant to your company and call or write for information.

Librarians

Before you leave the library, speak to the business or reference librarian. Explain that you are researching a small, local company and ask for suggestions about outside information contacts. The librarian probably has considerable experience in researching companies and undoubtedly has had opportunities to assist other people investigating local firms. Because of this familiarity with the community and its businesses, the librarian may be able to suggest several useful contacts for a local firm.

STATE GOVERNMENT OFFICES

While state government agencies have data about local companies in their records, it may take extra effort on your part to locate and obtain such information. Before you begin packing for a research visit to your state capital, however, be aware that you will not find concise evaluations that briefly profile a company and contain all the facts you desire. Rather, the available information will be widely scattered, and your findings may be incomplete, perhaps inconclusive, and frequently out of date. Because it may be difficult to find out exactly what is available without visiting an office, travel may be necessary. If you don't examine the material but merely request copies of anything with some bearing on a company, be prepared to receive documents that may have little or no research value. In other words, this approach to research, in addition to requiring time, effort, and some expense, will certainly have mixed returns. Before you start down this path, weigh the possible results and how necessary they are to your evaluation.

Despite this rather gloomy outlook, what avenues might you profitably explore in state records? Start by asking yourself what agencies have an interest in the facts you are trying to uncover. Determine the records these agencies have available and their probable content. Then examine the relevant materials at the office or request copies.

Financial Records

Financial data, for example, are often at the top of a company information wish list. One place to search for that data is in the corporate filings required by all states. Every corporation resident in a state, whether publicly or privately owned, must file an annual report with the appropriate state office. However, in nearly 80 percent of the states, this annual report is merely a registration form containing no more than company name, address, and chief officers. If a company happens to be located in one of the 10 or 12 states that asks for more data, you may learn the company's assets, the value of its property, any stock issued and its value, the value of the firm's inventory, and perhaps additional financial data.

You will find a brief description of the data that each state requires in these corporate annual reports in *Competitor Intelligence* by Leonard M. Fuld (John Wiley & Sons, 1985) described earlier in Chapter 7. Another possibility is to check your state's own code of laws and regulations for its corporate filing requirements. Either approach will take only a few minutes and will be worth the time if your state is one that requires the reporting of additional data. To obtain a copy of a report, call or write the appropriate state office. Expect a modest fee for copying and a delay of several days for processing your request.

Other State Records

The state occupational safety agency may also have useful data on companies. Businesses may be routinely inspected for the safety of their premises; manufacturers may be inspected for the safety of machinery and processes. The appropriate state office keeps inspection records on file as well as reports of on-the-job accidents; these records are open for examination by the public. Although the records may not be current, you can discover the safety record of a company or learn about the equipment and manufacturing processes used in factories.

Health and environmental inspections are another possibility. Any company that handles food products will be subject to health inspections. A report on a food processor may reveal details about equipment, plant operation, and manufacturing processes. These inspection reports will be open to the public. Environmental inspections may include any company whose manufacturing or operating processes create a potential for air, water, or ground pollution. Again, the records should be open for review in the appropriate state offices. Don't overlook the state consumer protection agency: Companies whose products or services are the target of persistent consumer complaint will be on record in that office with details of the problems encountered and remedial action taken.

A telephone call to the state employment agency may reveal a company's hiring practices. You may be able to determine how many positions are currently open, if hiring is seasonal in nature, whether layoffs are a frequent occurrence, and even if salaries are consistent with local averages. The best place to obtain answers to such questions may be the nearest regional or local office of the state employment agency, if there is one. They will be most familiar with companies in their locality and better able to answer specific questions.

Access to State Records

As a rule, try regional or local offices first for answers to any questions directed to state agencies. They will be smaller, more familiar with local companies, and may offer more service in person than you can obtain by telephone to the central state office. Check the state government listings in your local telephone book for suggestions.

A final word about information gathering in state government offices: On the plus side, nearly all state records are open to the public; there will be few, if any, restrictions on access. On the minus side is the difficulty encountered in identifying pertinent records and obtaining copies. It is easy to forget that the records are meant for state government use and are filed to provide access for state employees in their officially assigned responsibilities. Procedures will vary from state to state, but a search for company information may be easier if your requests are phrased in terms understood by the state service provider. Be as specific as possible and be patient. Your efforts will pay off in the end.

LOCAL AGENCIES

Even a company with a low profile in its community may leave a paper trail in local agencies. Telephone calls or visits to local offices may provide facts about a company not available elsewhere. In local offices, however, the potential problems outlined for state agencies also may exist. Data has been gathered for official use, not for its value in evaluating a company as an employer. Expect to find facts scattered, somewhat dated, and perhaps incomplete. An advantage, however, is that the records are geographically more centralized. You can visit the offices in person to examine files, and supplementary information may be available from other sources in the community.

Government Offices

Local government offices may contain information similar to that of state government agencies. Depending on your community's form of government, you may have separate city and county offices or combined offices under a metropolitan government. Access should generally be open. Administrative policies will vary, but remember that staff are rarely available to do research for you.

Among the local offices to visit are the following: the tax office or finance department for records of business or property taxes paid; the business office for permits to carry on business activity; the planning department for construction plans or zoning permits; the health department for safety or health inspection reports; the employment or labor department for job openings, hiring practices, and salary averages; and the consumer department for complaints about products and services.

Exact names of the responsible offices vary from community to community. If you are not sure where to begin, make a list of the facts you seek. Choose one office as a beginning point and obtain any available data there. Then ask for advice about the office that would have the next item on your list.

Industrial Development Boards

Many cities have an economic or industrial development board that develops commercial and industrial sites, works to attract new businesses to the area, and assists existing businesses in expansion or relocation projects. If a company has recently moved into the area or expanded its existing site, the development board may have a comprehensive file on it with information helpful to your evaluation. The board may not be willing to open its files to you, but speak to a representative about the company and ask for his or her opinions on its employment outlook.

Chambers of Commerce

Local chamber of commerce offices should be a first stop for information. Often regarded as a "booster" organization that promotes the city, the chamber also plays an important function in attracting new businesses and providing services to those companies already resident in the area. As a result, chamber officials are well acquainted with community businesses and can speak knowledgeably about their activities and outlook. If the chamber was active in recruiting a company into the area, officials may also be familiar with the firm's background and have insights into its future plans and priorities. If the company you are researching is a chamber member, its top executives may be known by chamber officials. The chamber may also have information available about the general business and employment outlook in your community and surrounding area. You are unlikely to be given free access to office files, but most chamber staff members are happy to assist business researchers. Call ahead for an appointment, explain the purpose of your visit, and ask to meet with the chamber representative most familiar with the company you are researching.

Better Business Bureaus

Another agency located in many cities is the Better Business Bureau (BBB). The BBB has served for many years as a clearinghouse for complaints of poor consumer goods and services. Companies reported to the BBB are notified of the complaints and have an opportunity to rectify the situation. Both the complaint and the company's response are kept on file at the BBB. A nationwide network allows local BBB offices to keep abreast of complaints from across the country. The BBB offices have information only on companies that have been the target of complaints. If a company has not been reported, little if any data will be available. If complaints have been made, the available information will deal with the disputed product or service and the company's response. Such reports may provide insight into the quality of a company's product or service.

You may want to investigate beyond the BBB's files to determine whether the company took steps to improve or change the product after settling the complaint. Response to complaints may also reveal a company's attitude toward its customers. If it treats customers fairly and with respect when a problem arises, a company may treat its employees in the same manner. A word of caution: Don't assume a complaint on file with the BBB means the customer was right. Despite its best efforts, a company may have been unable to satisfy a customer without the BBB's intervention. Get the full story about any complaint so that you may judge a company fairly.

Local Media

A final information-gathering suggestion, but an important one for local companies, is the local media. Both newspapers and broadcast media may be able to add to your information about a company. The value of scanning a local newspaper for recent articles about a company and its activities was noted earlier. You might also contact the business editor or reporter at the newspaper. Reporters usually know more about a subject than they can cover in print and may be excellent background sources.

When local businesses are their usual assignment, reporters will be well informed about specifics—who's hiring or expanding, the firms considered to be the best workplaces, why an executive is highly regarded by his peers or his staff, who is overextended financially—as well as about the general community economic outlook. If a reporter does not know your company well, ask about its local competitors or for suggestions and opinions of other highly regarded employers in the area. A local television station may not have a reporter assigned exclusively to business stories, but a general reporter may have additional information if a company has been the subject of recent coverage.

Take full advantage of the local sources available for researching a small company. Despite the extra time required and the need to visit several separate offices, information is usually reliable, service is generally fast, and people are almost always helpful.

Use offices and agencies for information about:

- Facilities
- Company Size
- Financial Data
- Company History
- Response to Difficulty
- Employee Morale

PEOPLE AS INFORMATION RESOURCES

People are always good sources of supplementary information, no matter what type of company you are researching. When you are investigating a small, local company, the value of people as primary sources of information dramatically increases. Only very exceptional small companies are profiled or evaluated in business publications commonly available in libraries. Information in government offices is scattered, sometimes inconvenient to obtain, and often out of date. On the other hand, personal contacts can provide timely, specific information directly relevant to your questions about a company. But who would make good contacts?

Personal Contacts

An obvious choice as a contact is someone already employed by the company. If you have a professional colleague, a friend, or family member in that position, you should have little trouble in learning about the company as a prospective employer. If you do not have immediate friends or family who are employees, perhaps an alumnus of your college, a fellow church member, or neighbor is. Any of these people should be excellent sources on the workplace atmosphere, salary levels, management personalities, and the quality of products and services. Your contacts may not be in a position, however, to know the financial and competitive status of the company or its long-term strategic plans. Also, their opinions will be colored by their own work experiences. Talk to them about the company—they are excellent sources on the topics they know—but balance their views with additional information from others.

Competitors, Suppliers, and Customers

If you do not have personal contacts within the company, consider contacting representatives of companies that work for or in competition with the one you are researching. Local competitors will have a good estimate of the level of a company's business, recent developments in products and markets, advertising strategies, the manager's style, the economic outlook—any area where the two companies come directly into contact. A supplier to a company will have information based on materials supplied for a manufacturing process or a retail operation.

Distributors of the company's products can provide insights on the volume of business, customer relations, and market outlook. Customers will focus on the service and the quality of products they have received. Chapter 4 discusses techniques for evaluating a company's products and services, and these may suggest additional options for evaluating a small local company. Notice, if possible, how a company advertises its products locally and get copies of any catalogs or promotional literature.

Local Association Members

Civic and professional associations are another possibility. The chamber of commerce is one of the best-known organizations of this type; its value as an information resource was discussed earlier. Most communities have a number of other business organizations. For example, local tourism, hotel, and restaurant managers may meet regularly to discuss common concerns. Minority business owners, representatives of companies located in a certain industrial park, women engineers—any group may have a regular meeting time or an office, providing you an opportunity to meet professionals and ask questions about a company. Ask at the local library, newspaper office, or chamber of commerce for assistance in identifying such groups.

Writers and Reporters

The potential value of information from a local business reporter has already been noted. If articles about a company have appeared in trade magazines or regional business magazines, note the byline author and any other individuals named in the articles. These people may also be potential contacts with specific insights into aspects of a company you are researching.

Trade Association Staff

Trade associations have been mentioned as a source of industry information but they rarely provide detailed information on individual companies. If the association membership is small, however, and a company is a leader in that group, a trade association representative may have personal knowledge of the company and its top managers and professionals. When you call the association offices to request industry data, ask if anyone can provide personal insight into the company you are researching.

Labor Union Representatives

Don't overlook the labor union. If a company is unionized, you may not be expected to join the union representing the workers, but you may be supervising workers who are union members and you will want to know how they view the company. Call the local union office for an additional viewpoint on the workplace. Union representatives can speak knowledgeably about local wage rates, working conditions, and management attitudes. Check the yellow pages of your local telephone directory under "Labor Organizations" for the union office. You may also use this directory:

Directory of U.S. Labor Organizations. Bureau of National Affairs Books. Annual.

> Provides a list of all unions affiliated with the AFL-CIO and all other major independent unions, their addresses, and top officials. In addition, it lists the names of contacts at AFL-CIO headquarters, state federations, and local offices.

The *Encyclopedia of Associations* (Gale Research Inc., annual), described in more detail in Chapter 4, also lists union organizations and provides the address and telephone number of the national headquarters.

Use personal contacts for information about:

- Facilities
- Product/Service
- Financial Data
- Company History
- Company Strategies
- Response to Difficulty
- Management/Employee Data
- Executive Biography
- Employee Morale
- Salaries
- Industry Outlook

INTERVIEWING AN INFORMATION SOURCE

To use the suggestions in the preceding section of this chapter, you must ask people questions. This may seem to be a simple task that you have been doing instinctively all your life. But when you are seeking information, a simple "yes," "no," or "maybe" response is not enough. You want to elicit details and facts from your source, together with personal observations and opinions. Mastery of a few basic interviewing skills can turn a brief, unproductive conversation into a fruitful, multifaceted interview. The tips that follow are not meant to turn you into an investigative reporter, only a successful company researcher.

Do your homework before you begin interviewing. Find out all that you can from published resources and make good notes to get your background data together. You may even find that you have all you need to evaluate a prospective employer without making any calls. Once your background facts are in order, create a list of key questions. Jot them down on a pad with plenty of space between so that you can take brief notes of the answers during an interview. You may even want to prepare a simple script that you can use to explain the purpose of your call or visit. Take care during the interview, however, not to follow a script too closely. If the conversation moves into an unexpected but useful area, you want to be prepared to depart from your script and explore that topic.

Draw up a list of possible contacts, but before you begin, decide which ones are potentially the most valuable. You are probably going to make mistakes in your first interview attempts—forget an important question or explain the purpose of your call awkwardly. Start with sources where you can afford to slip up and save the most important interviews until you are comfortable and have sufficient background information. Plan to talk to at least three or four people. Each contact will have his or her own point of view about a company, based on personal experience and knowledge. Hearing the assessments of several different people will provide a more accurate and complete picture.

Use information-gathering interviews to practice manners and demeanor for an employment interview. Whether calling for information or only to request an interview, be open about the reason for your call. If you are turned down, don't give up or get angry. Ask, instead, for suggestions of someone else to call or another office to visit. When you begin an interview, explain again the reason for your call or visit. The better the person you are speaking to understands the purpose of your questions, the better he or she can respond. Be polite and respectful and try to win the other person's support for your research effort. Most people will be flattered to be asked for advice and glad to assist you.

Be a good listener. Answers to your inquiries may suggest additional questions. Also, listen carefully to the nuances behind words you hear: Subtle warnings about a company may be phrased in politely superficial expressions. Practice taking notes while listening so that you don't lose the thread of a discussion. If you decide to tape an interview, ask for permission. Remember, however, that comments may be less open when you tape responses. Be considerate of the interviewee's time. If you have a number of lengthy requests or questions for a telephone interview, ask if you are calling at a convenient time. If you are interviewing in person, be sure to cover all your important questions within your allotted time. *Always* ask for referrals to others who might have additional information. Finally, don't forget to thank the people who have helped you.

PART III

RESEARCHING SPECIAL TOPICS

9 Finding Out about Salaries

Everyone wants to know about salaries when researching a company. Does the firm offer fair salaries for the work expected? Are they at or above average for the position offered? How do they compare with the going rate, either nationally or locally? How can you find a ballpark figure that will show whether a company meets the norms set by others in its industry or geographic area? In fact, actual salary rates for specific positions with an individual company are difficult to identify and are often subject to error and lack of currency. But no matter what type of company you are researching, data on representative salary levels for comparative purposes are fairly easy to find.

LIBRARY SOURCES

Books

Your initial impulse when starting your library research may be to look for a book containing salary data. Books, however, are seldom the best source for such information. By the time a book is published and available, its data may no longer be current.

Also, any book has to take into account a broad spectrum of work conditions and local variations in cost of living. To portray this diversity accurately, a book must quote a broad salary range for any position. This range can vary by several thousand dollars, making comparisons with actual job offers difficult.

With this caution in mind, you may still want to look at one or two books to get a rough idea of salary ranges. Two possible sources are:

John W. Wright and Edward J. Dwyer. *The American Almanac of Jobs and Salaries.* Avon. 1990.

> This book contains pay rates for hundreds of occupations around the United States. Jobs surveyed range from white-collar and professional to technical and blue-collar positions. It usually gives an average salary range for the occupation, plus salaries for some specific positions. Updated every two to three years, this is a good source of what to expect as an average salary around the nation.

American Salaries and Wages Survey, 1st ed. Gale Research Inc. 1991.

> Salary data are provided for over 4,500 occupations at different experience levels and in specific areas of the country. Data is extracted from publications issued by government offices, professional organizations, and periodicals and newspapers. Good for actual representative salaries, but figures found here are quickly out of date.

Other sources of entry level salary data are also available. Among them are the *Occupational Outlook Handbook* (U.S. Bureau of Labor Statistics, biennial) and *The Encyclopedia of Careers and Vocational Guidance* (J.G. Ferguson Publishing Co., 8th ed., 1990). Both provide broad salary ranges and average earnings for several hundred occupations; see Chapter 11 for a full description of their other features. *Geographic Reference* (BTA Economic Research Institute, annual), a statistical overview described in more detail in Chapter 10, compares demographic and economic conditions in over 250 U.S. and Canadian cities and provides salary data for specific locations. It has estimates of median annual salaries paid in each city for about 75 occupations, blue collar to professional.

In employment guides such as the *CPC Annual* (College Placement Council, annual), major companies describe their job opportunities for college graduates, including a brief outline of company salaries and benefits. *Dun's Employment Opportunities Directory/The Career Guide* (Dun & Bradstreet Information Services, annual) and *The National Job Bank* (Bob Adams, Inc., annual) are two more examples containing similar brief summaries of company benefits. All three of these employment guides are described in more detail in Chapter 13. In fact, any book on careers may include an estimate of the salary range expected for a particular occupation.

The U.S. Bureau of Labor Statistics (BLS) publishes a variety of wage survey reports each year. Some of these, the *Occupational Compensation Surveys* (formerly *Area Wage Surveys),* cover specific metropolitan areas; others, such as the *Industry Wage Surveys,* look at occupational wages within a single industry. The occupations surveyed, however, are primarily clerical, technical, or mechanical; only a very few administrative positions are included. *White Collar Pay,* another BLS publication, also focuses primarily on clerical jobs. There is generally a two-year lag between federal data collection and publication. Although useful for some purposes, more current sources of salary information are available elsewhere.

Periodicals and Newspapers

For up-to-date salary information, periodicals are usually a better choice than books. Periodicals often conduct annual salary surveys. For example, *Working Woman* has a survey of business and professional women's salaries every January. *Inc.* magazine reviews executive compensation annually in its September issue.

For salary trends in a specific field, look at a trade journal. They frequently carry national salary surveys for their industry or profession. *Hospitals,* for example, has an annual survey of hospital executives salaries and incentive pay. *Chemical and Engineering News* annually surveys the compensation of chemists and engineers. Many such surveys provide salary averages for several geographical regions and for various levels of experience. *Sales & Marketing Management,* for example, publishes a special issue in February each year called "Survey of Selling Costs" with data on compensation of sales staff, sales incentives, and travel costs around the nation.

Although many surveys are available annually, others appear far less frequently. If you are searching for a salary survey published irregularly or in a field not covered by a trade journal, try a general business periodical. An index such as *Business Periodicals Index* (H. W. Wilson Co., monthly) is a good place to start tracking an occasional survey. (You'll find a description of its features in Chapter 4.) Many of the specialized trade journals are not indexed; you may need help locating their salary surveys. If a salary survey is a recurring feature of a periodical, a librarian may be able to locate it for you by checking an index of special issues of periodicals.

For examples of representative salary data that are more specific than a survey, scan the ads for current job openings in trade and professional journals and newsletters. Many libraries carry job advertisement reprint services such as the *National Business Employment Weekly,* which contains the large block ads for jobs from all the regional editions of *The Wall Street Journal.* Your library may also carry out-of-town newspapers with extensive help wanted sections. Salary minimums are often listed for the positions in these publications. Even if the position listed is not one you intend to apply for, you can get an idea of what you might expect to earn if the training and experience required is similar to yours.

Don't forget that many of the positions listed in these sources are advertised nationally, and the employer is often a major corporation. When comparing salaries with a job offered by a small local company, you may find appreciable differences in salary rates. Differences may also occur in communities where the cost of living is markedly higher or lower than the national average. In either case, compare the salary with others in the local area to get a true comparison.

SALARY INFORMATION OUTSIDE THE LIBRARY

If you have exhausted the salary information resources of your library, you can explore other sources for representative examples.

Placement Centers

Start at your college placement service if you are a student. That office will have records of salaries offered to previous graduates in your field that you can use for comparison. It will also have job listings for current openings locally and around the country that will indicate entry level salaries.

Employment Offices

Call or write your state employment office; often this agency has an office in each county. Its address and telephone number are listed in the state government pages of your telephone book. The employment office will have a list of current job openings, usually stating a salary minimum. The office may also have data on average salary levels in your state and county. If you are interested in a local employer, counselors in the office may have personal knowledge of the company and its salary rates, whether jobs are currently listed or not. If you are considering an out-of-state employer, call or write the employment office of the appropriate state for information. Assistance to out-of-state inquiries may be limited, however, as state residents usually have priority.

Private employment agencies may also be able to assist you. Most do not reveal the specific salary for job openings they have available unless you are a serious candidate for the position. There are always exceptions, however, and most private employment counselors will be glad to look at a copy of your resume and briefly discuss job opportunities and salary ranges.

Trade Unions

Trade unions may also be able to provide salary information. If a company is unionized, the union office has data on compensation and benefits for employees covered under the union contract. Although the union is not involved with salary negotiations for nonunion employees (generally the white-collar and management-level positions), union officials often have a good idea of salary ranges and company benefits for all employees.

Personal Contacts

Get in touch with your personal contacts. Although many people are reluctant to discuss their own salary, they are almost always happy to speculate about others. If you have developed a network of contacts in your field over the years, now is the time to call them. Ask what colleagues with experience and responsibilities similar to yours are currently being paid. Don't overlook the equally important factor of periodic salary increases. If you have contacts within the company, ask what the usual increase is, how often it is given, and the performance factors weighed in salary decisions.

Salary data are elusive, but such information is only one factor to consider when evaluating a prospective employer. Don't be disappointed if you cannot locate specifics, either in library resources or from personal contacts. Use the information you do find, look at how a company measures up in all other categories, and base your evaluation on the composite data.

10 Finding the Best Place to Live and Work

Relocation is often a deciding factor in searching for a job. Location may be as important a motive as a top-notch salary or an industry-leading employer. You may have visited an area and want to return there to live and work. Or you may simply want a change of scene and the excitement of living in a new city. Before you move, however, research your new location. You may find that the sun doesn't shine every day as it did on your vacation or that the economic outlook for the area is bleak. Even if location is not at the top of your list of factors to consider when researching an employer, knowing about a city may pay off. It may make the choice between two apparently equal job opportunities easier, and it may prevent a long-distance move if you discover that your hometown is the only place where you can be happy.

RESEARCHING NEW LOCATIONS AT THE LIBRARY

In addition to being the easiest place to begin researching a company, the library is also a good place to start researching a new location. Find background information there, plus guides to additional resources. If you are doing your research in a college library, visit the public library, too, because it may have a larger collection of travel and descriptive materials.

Weather Records

Look first at the climate and geography of an area. Is it hot and humid nine months of the year? Are air pollution levels a national scandal? Do nearby mountains and lakes make the area a vacationer's paradise? Such questions are easy to answer. Start by looking at the weather. A U.S. government publication containing weather data is:

Climatological Data. U.S. National Climatic Data Center. Monthly.

> This record of weather conditions at various reporting stations in each state notes temperature and precipitation, along with wind, days and hours of sunshine, cloud cover, and weather type. A companion series called *Local Climatological Data* provides similar facts for major metropolitan areas throughout the United States.

Weather information may also be found in this publication:

Weather of U.S. Cities, 4th ed. Gale Research Inc. 1989.

> Weather records for 281 cities in the United States and its island territories are gathered into this volume. A narrative description of climate characteristics for each city outlines typical weather conditions throughout the year. Detailed statistical tables provide monthly weather summaries and a 30-year weather history for each location.

Maps and Atlases

An area's geographic setting can be determined in several sources. Maps are a good place to begin. Start with a road atlas and look up the state you are interested in. Try this well-known atlas for example:

Rand McNally Road Atlas. Rand McNally & Co. Annual.

State maps show the major highways, roads, and cities, and also indicate the location of parks, campsites, national forests, lakes, rivers, and mountain peaks. The index gives population figures for cities and counties.

A variation on the road atlas is:

Commercial Atlas and Marketing Guide. Rand McNally & Co. Annual.

This atlas has large state maps showing the location of even the smallest population centers. Roads are not indicated—only railway lines. The indexes to the maps provide facts about population and transportation facilities in each locality. In addition, the atlas contains statistical tables with data ranging from population and income to retail sales and car registration for counties and for cities with populations over 25,000.

For more geographical features, browse through a library's atlas and map collection. Maps that portray special types of geographical data such as physical features, climate, geology, land use, natural resources, or vegetation are commonly available. For a close-up look at the physical features of a specific area, ask if the library carries the "quadrangle" maps of the U.S. Geological Survey, which have been prepared for the entire United States and come in several scales, the most common being the 1:24000 or 7.5 scale. This means that each map, or quadrangle, equals 7.5 minutes of latitude and longitude of the earth's surface. At this scale, contours—variations in altitude and terrain—are clearly marked at 20-foot levels; and both man-made and natural features such as roads, bridges, streams, hills, and footpaths are easily located.

Guidebooks

Tourist or visitor guides make interesting browsing. Most libraries have a selection and many additional titles can be purchased in bookstores. Here's one example:

Mobil Travel Guides. Prentice-Hall. Annual.

A series of regional guides published annually covering the 48 continental United States. Each guide has travel planning data for individual localities in the states. The history of each community is briefly noted and major cultural and recreational attractions are listed.

Many libraries also have the state travel guides of the famous *American Guide Series,* prepared in the late 1930s by the Works Projects Administration of the federal government. Although most volumes in the series are over 50 years old, each provides a rich portrait of the history, culture, and byways of a state. Read them not as tour guides, but as introductions to the character and mood of the state you are researching. A more up-to-date view is found in this set:

Cities of the United States. Gale Research Inc. 1988–1989.

Divided geographically into South, West, Midwest, and Northeast, the four volumes of this set cover about 130 of the nation's largest and fastest growing cities. Each city's profile is based on data from a number of sources and covers its history, geography, government, economy, and society.

Another widely available source providing city facts is:

World Almanac. Pharos Books. Annual.

It surveys about 100 major metropolitan areas, noting each city's vital statistics, history, facilities, and chamber of commerce address in a brief paragraph.

Statistics

Visitor information usually looks at only one aspect of a city—the fun and excitement of its attractions. For another side of the picture, look at statistics. The most meaningful use of statistics is to compare your present location with the city you are considering. By making comparisons, you can see if the new city is really bigger, wealthier, and cleaner—or only looks that way to a casual visitor.

Statistics for cities are available in many sources. Begin with publications of the U.S. government:

Statistical Abstract of the United States. U.S. Bureau of the Census. Annual.

> Available in all libraries, this volume is a first stop for statistical questions because it serves both as a primary source for data and as a guide to additional information. Although most tables survey the United States as a whole, regional, state, and metropolitan data are included.

County and City Data Book. U.S. Bureau of the Census. Irregular.

> This companion volume to the *Statistical Abstract* is published every four to five years. It contains comparative statistics for U.S. counties and cities in a variety of demographic, social, and economic categories. Topics such as crime, education, employment, and housing are easy to compare in various cities by using the tables found here. It is also available in some libraries in compact disc format (see Figure 10.1).

Much data in the *Statistical Abstract* and all of that in the *County and City Data Book* are derived from U.S. census surveys. Federal census publications are the chief source of comprehensive statistical data on the nation. They also provide extensive data on individual states, counties, metropolitan areas, and cities. Every 10 years, the federal government undertakes a census of population and housing, counting all residents and gathering social and economic data. The most recent census population count was taken in 1990. In addition, a series of economic censuses is taken every five years enumerating business and industry. Census data are available in many libraries; significant portions of the 1990 population census and the economic censuses are available for use in compact disc format.

Most states publish a statistical handbook or abstract that contains data about their local area. The state data are usually derived from U.S. census publications and other federal

Table C. Cities — **Police Officers, Education, Money Income**

City	Police officers, 1985		Educational attainment,[2] 1980		Money income					
					Per capita[3]				Percent below poverty level, 1979	
					1985		1979			
	Number	Rate[1]	Percent completing 12 years or more	Percent completing 16 years or more	Total (Dol.)	Percent of State average	Current dollars	Constant (1985) dollars	Persons	Families
	32	33	34	35	36	37	38	39	40	41
INDIANA	X	X	66.4	12.5	9 978	100.0	7 141	10 583	9.7	7.3
Anderson	NA	NA	61.5	10.7	10 173	102.0	6 843	10 141	12.7	10.0
Bloomington	55	10.3	82.3	47.8	8 513	85.3	5 804	8 602	23.3	11.1
Columbus	62	20.0	69.7	18.9	12 005	120.3	8 443	12 513	10.6	8.1
East Chicago	98	25.4	44.9	5.5	7 905	79.2	6 499	9 632	16.8	15.9
Elkhart	96	23.4	65.2	13.7	10 194	102.2	7 196	10 664	12.0	9.2
Evansville	231	17.7	61.1	11.2	10 048	100.7	7 040	10 433	12.2	8.5
Fort Wayne	308	18.6	68.7	13.3	10 276	103.0	7 049	10 447	11.0	8.5
Gary	273	19.1	55.0	7.6	7 488	75.0	6 170	9 144	20.4	18.0

Figure 10.1 Typical entries, reprinted from the *County and City Data Book,* 1988 edition, published by the U.S. Bureau of the Census.

documents as well as various state publications. Occasionally additional statistics or surveys not available elsewhere are published in the state compendia. Most libraries will have the statistical handbook for their state.

Market Guides

In addition to federal and state statistical publications, commercially published market guides provide consumer market data for communities across the nation. Although intended for use by sales and marketing professionals, these community profiles are also valuable to anyone gathering information about a city. Although based in part on U.S. census data, several publications prepare their own estimates of demographic and market data to supplement and update the federal statistics. Among the most widely available of these publications is:

The Survey of Buying Power Demographics USA. Sales & Marketing Management Magazine. Annual.

> The data in this consumer market survey appears initially in special July and October issues of *Sales & Marketing Management* magazine and is later published with additions in this annual survey. Here are detailed population, household, and retail sales data in addition to market data projections, disposable personal income estimates, and a buying power index. Statistics are available for the United States as a whole, and for states, metropolitan areas, counties, and television viewing markets. While U.S. census data are often several years out of date, *Demographics USA* provides reliable current estimates to illustrate the present economic status of a city.

A market data source emphasizing the city rather than its demographics is:

Editor & Publisher Market Guide. Editor and Publisher. Annual.

> Find statistical and market data for over 1,600 U.S. and Canadian cities with a daily newspaper in this volume. Included for each city are location, population, major industries, banks, utilities, retailing and retail outlets such as shopping centers and chain stores, transportation facilities, climate, and newspapers. Also included are statistics and rankings of cities by income, population, and retail sales (see Figure 10.2).

Cost-of-Living Estimates

Few questions about a new city are more important than cost of living. Cost-of-living questions frequently are phrased as questions about the "Consumer Price Index." Almost everyone has heard of the federal Consumer Price Index, but few are clear about what it is. Briefly, it is a U.S. government measure of inflation that tracks changes in price levels over time and is based on the prices of commonly purchased consumer goods and services. The index is reported for the nation as a whole and for 27 major cities.

While valuable as a gauge of inflationary increases, the federally produced CPI cannot be used to compare cost of living between cities. It measures change over time within a single area, not the comparative difference between areas. A good source of cost-of-living data for comparison between cities is:

KALAMAZOO

1—LOCATION: Kalamazoo County (MSA). E&P Map C-5, County Seat. Industrial, wholesale & educational center. On U.S. Hwy. 131, I-94 & State Hwy. M-43; 141 mi. E of Chicago; 142 mi. W of Detroit.

2—TRANSPORTATION: Railroads-Conrail; Grand Trunk; Amtrak.
Motor Freight Carriers-22.
Intercity Bus Lines-Greyhound; Indian Trails; Indiana Motor; Short-Way.
Airlines-Northwest; Piedmont; Air Wisconsin; American Eagle; United.

3—POPULATION:
Corp. City 80 Cen. 79,722; E&P 88 Est. 76,307
CZ-ABC: (80) 148,436
RTZ-ABC: (80) 183,133
County/**MSA** 80 Cen. 212,581; E&P 88 Est. 218,153
City & RTZ-ABC: (80) 331,569

4—HOUSEHOLDS:
City 80 Cen. 28,375; E&P 88 Est. 28,578
County/**MSA** 80 Cen. 75,405; E&P 88 Est. 78,929
CZ-ABC: (80) 53,022
RTZ-ABC: (80) 63,648
City & RTZ-ABC: (80) 116,670

5—BANKS	**NUMBER**	**DEPOSITS**
Savings	9	$1,279,846,000
Savings & Loan	3	$629,546,000

6—PASSENGER AUTOS: County 132,979

7—ELECTRIC METERS: Residence 131,298

8—GAS METERS: Residence 64,271

9—PRINCIPAL INDUSTRIES: Industry, No. of Wage Earners-Paper & Allied Prods. 4,700; Chem. & Allied Prods. 7,200; Metal 5,500; Constr. 3,800; Trans. Equip. 2,900; Average wages for all industries ($404).

10—CLIMATE: Min. & Max. Temp.-Spring 34-67; Summer 60-80; Fall 31-45; Winter 16-31. First killing frost, Oct. 9; last killing frost, May 16.

11—TAP WATER: Alkaline, very hard; fluoridated.

12—RETAILING: Principal Shopping Center-7 blocks on Michigan Ave.; 6 on Burdick St.
Neighborhood Shopping Centers-Portage at Lovers Lane; E. Main at Nazareth Rd.; W. Main at Drake Rd.; Portage at Paddington; Portage at Bloomfield; Shoppers' Lane, Parchment; S. Westnedge at Milham Rd.; I-94 at Portage; S. Westnedge at Kilgore; Maple Hill Mall; W. Main Mall; Crossroads Mall; E. Towne Mall.

Nearby Shopping Centers

Name (No. of stores)	**Miles from Downtown**	**Principal Stores**
Airport Plaza (3)	4	Zayre
Bloomfield Plaza (22)	NA	Stop-N-Go Foods
Cork-Lane (9)	2	Rite Aid, Libin's Men's Store
Eastwood Plaza (11)	NA	Rite Aid
Kalamazoo Ctr. Fashion Mall (30)	NA	Hallmark Cards, The Greenery
Kalamazoo Mall (55)	NA	Jacobson's, Walgreens, Gilmore's
Maple Hill Mall (70)	NA	Mont. Ward, Gilmore's, Meijer's
Southland Mall (30)	NA	Highland Appliance, T.J. Maxx, Gilmore's
Westmain Mall (55)	NA	Zayre
Crossroads Mall	NA	JCPenney, Sears, Hudson's

Principal Shopping Days-Sat., Sun., Wed., & Fri.
Stores Open Evenings-Wed.; some also on Fri.; some department stores 6 nights weekly; all malls every evening.

13—RETAIL OUTLETS: Department Stores-Gilmore Bros. 3; Sears; JCPenney; Jacobson's; Wards; Steketees; Hudson's; Hills.
Variety Stores-G.L. Perry.
Discount Stores-Zayre 2; Thrifty Acres 3; Osco 2; K mart 3; T.J. Maxx.
Chain Drug Stores-Walgreens; Perry 3; Rite Aid.
Chain Supermarkets-IGA 2; Spartan 8; Harding's 38; Meijer's 3; Jewel Food 3; Family Foods 4; Viking Foods.
Other Chain Stores-Fox's; Nobil; L.G. Haig; Firestone; Goodrich; Goodyear; Highland Appliance; Fretter Appliance; Quality Farm & Fleet 2; Toys "R" Us; Radio Shack 6; Frank's Nursery 2.

14—NEWSPAPERS: GAZETTE (e) 62,179; (S) 77,520. Mar. 31, 1988 ABC.
Local Contact for Advertising and Merchandising Data: James Pulliam, Dis. Adv. Mgr., GAZETTE, 401 S. Burdick St., Kalamazoo, MI 49003; Tel. (616) 345-3511.
National Representative: Newhouse Newspapers Metro Suburbia.

Figure 10.2 Typical entry, *Editor & Publisher Market Guide,* 1989 edition. Reprinted by permission.

Cost of Living Index. American Chamber of Commerce Researchers Association (ACCRA). Quarterly.

Data found here measure cost-of-living differences among a selected group of nearly 300 urban areas across the nation. Researchers from local chambers of commerce gather average retail prices in their locality for about 60 commonly used consumer goods and services. ACCRA computes a national average as a comparative index for all items and for six broad categories of purchases. The prices for each city are then computed as a percentage of the ACCRA index, as illustrated in Figure 10.3. Glancing at the tables can show quickly, for example, how costs will compare between cities such as Nashville, Tennessee, and Spokane, Washington. Part Two of the ACCRA report gives actual retail prices in each of the cities surveyed for specific items such as pizza, milk, movie tickets, or bus fares (see Figure 10.3).

Another method of checking prices is to browse issues of a city's newspaper. Reading the ads gives an approximate idea of local housing costs, grocery purchases, clothing, and a number of services.

Community Amenities

While you are making comparisons of living costs, what about comparing other community amenities such as schools, museums, and recreational facilities; or community issues such as crime, health services, and tax rates? Depending on the items of interest or concern to you, here is a sampler of resources. Your reference librarian may be able to offer additional suggestions.

Education

Patterson's American Education. Educational Directories, Inc. Annual.

> This directory provides the addresses of school systems and secondary schools in cities across the United States. Private secondary schools and postsecondary schools are also noted.

Handbook of Private Schools. Porter Sargent Publishers Inc. Annual.

> Details of privately supported educational facilities are presented. An index of special offerings indicates features such as military training, gifted and talented programs, or opportunities for international education.

ACCRA COST OF LIVING INDEX SECOND QUARTER 1991

COMPONENT INDEX WEIGHTS	100%	13%	28%	9%	10%	5%	35%
MSA/PHSA URBAN AREA AND STATE	COMPOSITE INDEX	GROCERY ITEMS	HOUSING	UTILITIES	TRANS-PORTATION	HEALTH CARE	MISC. GOODS AND SERVICES
Columbus OH MSA							
Columbus OH	108.9	100.7	115.8	109.4	121.3	105.0	103.9
Newark/Licking County OH	98.1	100.6	85.3	106.4	103.6	95.2	101.4
Dayton-Springfield OH MSA							
Dayton-Springfield OH	101.0	89.6	113.7	101.7	100.5	98.5	98.7
Mansfield OH MSA							
Mansfield OH	98.1	97.7	91.7	122.4	94.9	93.6	96.5
Parkersburg-Marietta WV-OH MSA							
Marietta OH	92.3	100.5	83.0	88.4	88.8	86.2	98.7
Youngstown-Warren OH MSA							
Youngstown OH	94.5	99.2	86.7	115.0	90.0	86.3	93.9
Nonmetropolitan Areas							
Ashland OH	96.8	97.4	87.0	126.9	86.5	91.7	98.1
Findlay OH	99.5	100.2	102.0	91.5	96.4	91.8	103.2
Mount Vernon/Knox County OH	96.3	105.7	89.8	107.7	99.4	88.6	91.9
Sandusky/Erie County OH	105.9	102.6	112.4	126.2	109.5	98.0	96.0

Figure 10.3 Typical entries, *Cost of Living Index*, 2nd quarter, 1991 edition. Copyright © 1991 by the American Chamber of Commerce Researchers Association. Reprinted by permission.

Health Care and Social Services

American Medical Directory. American Medical Association. Biennial.

Directory of Medical Specialists. Marquis Who's Who. Biennial.

Both directories list physicians by state and city. Both give brief biographical details of education, training, experience, and board certification of specialty.

Guide to the Health Care Field. American Hospital Association. Annual.

This guide lists and describes all hospitals in the United States, noting number of staff, beds, and special features such as intensive care units, burn treatment facilities, or trauma care centers.

Public Welfare Directory. American Public Welfare Association. Annual.

National Directory of Private Social Agencies. Social Service Publications. Monthly.

Both directories list and describe social services. The first lists those of federal and state governments and provides addresses, telephone numbers, and the names of key staff. The second contains those private agencies and organizations that provide direct services or make referrals.

Cultural Activities and Recreation

Musical America. ABC Publishing. Annual.

Subtitled the *International Directory of the Performing Arts,* it lists orchestras, opera companies, dance and choral groups, festivals, schools, and state arts agencies. A special feature is a survey of major metropolitan areas, noting the musical groups and performances scheduled in the city during the year.

Official Museum Directory. American Association of Museums. Annual.

Over 6,000 museums of all types are described. Art, history, and science predominate, but special museums such as those featuring stamps, sports, wax figures, comedy, theater, or toys are also included.

Michael Frome. *National Park Guide.* Prentice-Hall. Annual.

This is a complete guide to all national parks, monuments, wilderness areas, seashores and other facilities under the care of the U.S. National Park Service.

Chase's Annual Events. Contemporary Books. Annual.

Arranged day by day through the year, this is a list of national and state holidays, sponsored events and festivals, days denoted by presidential proclamation, historical events, and religious observances. An index by state and subject helps to locate events geographically or by special interest.

The Environment

Risks and Hazards: A State by State Guide. U.S. Federal Emergency Management Administration. 1990.

Maps illustrate the incidence and location of both natural and man-made hazards such as tornados, earthquakes, nuclear power plants, and hazardous dam sites across the United States.

Crime

Crime in the United States: Uniform Crime Reports. U.S. Federal Bureau of Investigation. Annual.

This report provides annual statistics on crime rates in states, counties, and cities over 10,000 in population. Data are provided on criminal offenses, persons arrested, and law enforcement personnel.

Sourcebook of Criminal Justice Statistics. U.S. Bureau of Justice Statistics. Annual.

Characteristics of the American criminal justice system are outlined through statistics on offenses, arrests, judicial processing, correctional service, and public attitudes. Data are given for states and for cities, where available.

Government and Taxes

The Municipal Year Book. International City Management Association. Annual.

This survey covers major issues facing cities such as affordable housing, solid waste disposal, and affirmative action. A number of comparative tables illustrate how cities are faring. A directory of top civic officials is included.

Book of the States. Council of State Governments. Annual.

Major issues facing state governments, such as taxation, reapportionment, social services, industrial development, state budgets, or the environment are briefly profiled. Innovative programs and creative solutions to problems are highlighted. Many tables show comparisons between states.

State Tax Guide. Commerce Clearing House. Annual with updates.

Rate information is provided for various taxes levied by states on items such as income, retail sales, gasoline, or tobacco. The name and address of each state tax commissioner are given if you wish to write for more information.

City Rankings

You may not have time to look at all the sources that compare the lifestyle and living conditions in various cities. Or you may want another opinion of a city to compare with your own. Consult one of several published comparative rankings of cities as an alternative. Remember however that the published rankings are based on priorities chosen by the authors, and these may be very different from your own. Also, some subjective choices are inevitable in the rankings, no matter what statistical measures are used. Consult the rankings as guides, but make a final decision about a city based on what is important to you. Among the best known of the comparative rankings are these:

Richard Boyer and David Savageau. *Places Rated Almanac: Your Guide to Finding the Best Places to Live in America,* 3rd ed. Prentice-Hall. 1989.

> This popular guide ranks over 300 major metropolitan areas according to individual criteria such as cost of living, job opportunities, educational facilities, health and the environment, safety, transportation, the arts, and climate. Each city also receives an overall ranking for these criteria.

G. Scott Thomas. *The Rating Guide to Life in America's Small Cities.* Promethus Books. 1990.

> The author surveys 219 cities that are not major metropolitan areas but have much to offer anyone who wants to escape big-city headaches. Each city is rated on standard factors such as the economy, education, health, climate, crime, and housing costs. In addition, each community is ranked for sophistication and urban proximity.

Geographic Reference. BTA Economic Research Institute. Annual.

> Subtitled "Annual Report of Costs, Wages, Salaries, and Human Resource Statistics," this survey looks at 265 major metropolitan areas in the United States and Canada and provides statistics for comparative purposes. Included are standard items such as climate, housing, health care, crime rates, and cost of living. More unusual items such as percentage of employment by industry, estimated median salaries for several dozen occupations, and estimated work-force demographics are also included (see Figure 10.4).

A few periodicals rate metropolitan areas on a regular basis. One example is *Money,* the popular periodical that provides advice on managing personal finances. It has published an annual ranked survey of America's 300 largest metropolitan areas for several years.

NASHVILLE, TENNESSEE

Nashville is located in north central Tennessee, on the Kentucky border, on bluffs overlooking the west bank of the Cumberland River. Nashville is the state capital, and is the seat of Davidson County.

Approx City Population 490,000
Approx MSA Population 1,013,000

Major products include aircraft wings and other parts, newspaper and printing, automobile and architectural glass, communications equipment, synthetic fibers, chemicals, shoes, apparel, processed meats, tires, trucks, grain and tobacco.

Employment % by Industry

Construction	6.1	Fin, Ins, & R.E.	8.3
Government	11.3	Manufacturing	14.9
Trade	22.9	Services	28.8
Trans & Utilities	5.0	Farming	2.4
		Mining	.2

Major Private Area Employers

Vanderbilt U & Medical	Opryland USA Inc
Kroger Company	HCA Healthcare
Nissan Motor Mfg	South Central Bell Co
Shoney's Incorporated	St Thomas Hospital
Service Merchandise Co	Baptist Hospital

Estimated Workforce Demographics

Age 16-19 6.2 % Age 20-44 63.8 % Age 45 + 30.0 %
Male 56.0 % Female 44.0 %
Unemployment 3.9 %

Weather

	Jan	Feb	Mar	Apr	May	Jun	Jul	Aug	Sep	Oct	Nov	Dec
Min Temp	29.	31.	38.	49.	57.	66.	69.	68.	61.	49.	38.	31.
Max Temp	48.	51.	59.	71.	80.	88.	90.	89.	84.	73.	59.	50.
Rainfall	4.8	4.4	5.0	4.1	4.1	3.4	3.8	3.2	3.1	2.2	3.5	4.5
Snowfall	4.2	3.2	1.7	.1	.0	.0	.0	.0	.0	.0	.8	2.0

Organized Labor Influence

Percentage Union Employees/All Employees 12.9 %

Area Crime Rate

Robberies	231.8/100,000	Homicides	9.0/100,000
Rapes	65.8/100,000	Assaults	549.4/100,000

Costs - Housing

Single 3 Bedroom, 2,000 sq ft Home $ 118238.
Comparable Rental - 3 Bedrooms $ 995./month

Costs - Hospital & Health Care

Average Daily Semiprivate Room Cost $ 207./day
Average Total Hospital Cost $ 579./day

Cost of Living Analyses v U.S. Average Level

	8,000	24,000	48,000	72,000
Housing/Utilts	1509.	6062.	15573.	27783.
Taxes Fd/St/Lc	0.	1704.	6240.	12240.
Consumables	3796.	7863.	11068.	12216.
Transportation	544.	2331.	3908.	4351.
Services/Other	1848.	4827.	8517.	10235.
% vs Total U.S.	96.%	95.%	94.%	93.%

Effective Income & Sales Tax Rates

Fd/St/Lc I Tax .0 % 7.0 % 13.0 % 17.0 %
Sales/Use Tax 7.75 %

Area Structures

	Cost of Living	Wage & Salary
$ 8,000 - $24,000	.943 x n + 151.	.882 x n + 1443.
$24,000 - $48,000	.938 x n + 268.	.945 x n - 70.
$48,000 & above	.897 x n + 2269.	1.052 x n - 5221.

("n" = U.S. National Earnings)

COMPARED TO THE U.S. NATIONAL AVERAGE

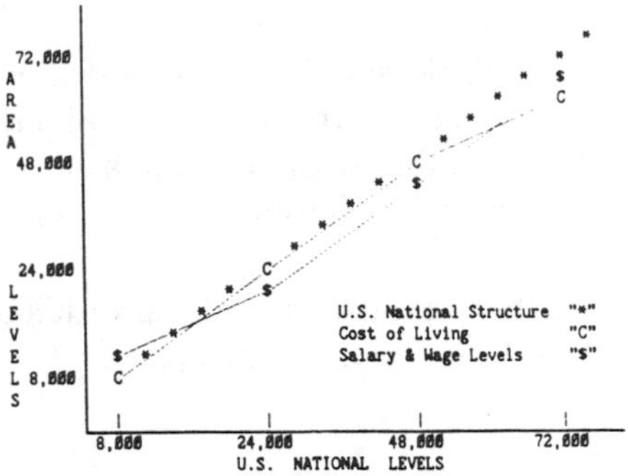

Institute Estimate of Annual Median Salaries

Accountant	30226.	Manufacturing Worker	15132.
Accounting Clerk	17094.	Market Analyst	31051.
Admin Assistant	23118.	Marketing Manager	43056.
Attorney (Staff)	49649.	Materials Handler	19136.
Auditor	31439.	Mechanic (Auto)	23633.
Bank Teller	13146.	Mechanic (Machinery)	24505.
Benefits Analyst	24466.	Messenger	13689.
Benefits Manager	32303.	Millwright	19460.
Biologist	30688.	Nurse (Registered)	25145.
Bookkeeper	20088.	Office Manager	31292.
Bus Driver	22019.	Order Clerk	16718.
Buyer/Purchasing Agent	24574.	Painter	18833.
Carpenter	23116.	Payroll Clerk	18774.
Chemist	38705.	PC Specialist	28991.
Computer Operator	19271.	Personnel Analyst	20953.
Construction Worker	22778.	Personnel Manager	43529.
Contract Administrator	34908.	Physician (Public)	65771.
Controller	39935.	Physicist	42416.
Cook (Company)	16498.	Plumber/Pipefitter	24738.
Corrections Officer	21904.	Programmer	29071.
Data Librarian	21076.	Programmer (Lead)	36998.
Dental Assistant	14905.	Purchasing Manager	30886.
Designer	29404.	Receptionist	15860.
Drafter	21708.	Sales Manager	38870.
EDP Director	44034.	Salesperson	23424.
Electrical Engineer	39704.	Secretary	19147.
Electronics Technician	22806.	Shipper & Receiver	20860.
Engineer (Stationary)	32403.	Shipping Clerk	16381.
Engineering Director	55028.	Statistician	30703.
Estimator	26206.	Supervisor	30574.
Executive Secretary	22848.	Surveyor	19565.
File Clerk	14060.	Switchboard Operator	16000.
Financial Analyst	30445.	Systems Analyst	35256.
Guard	21119.	Systems Analyst (Lead)	43604.
Helper - Maintenance	13268.	Teacher (Primary)	21132.
Investigator/Crime	33541.	Teacher (Secondary)	22136.
Janitor	15734.	Textile Worker	16282.
Key Entry Operator	14839.	Tool & Die Maker	24583.
Lab Technician	24250.	Truck Driver (Heavy)	23840.
Librarian	21035.	Truck Driver (Light)	21626.
Machine Tool Operator	21207.	Typist	15112.
Machinist	22815.	Uniformed Policeman	28117.
Maintenance Worker	14095.	Warehouse Worker	16940.
Manufacturing Director	36107.	Word Processor	17342.

160

Data as of: 1/ 1/91

Figure 10.4 Typical entry, *Geographic Reference,* 1990 edition. Reprinted by permission of BTA Economic Research Institute.

To compare states as well as cities, look at this publication:

Almanac of the 50 States. Information Publications. Annual.

This small volume provides a quick but thorough survey of each of the states. Also included are tables giving comparative rankings of the states on a variety of demographic and economic factors.

Other resources ranking cities and states are available; ask a librarian for suggestions.

WHAT'S AVAILABLE BEYOND THE LIBRARY?

Don't overlook information resources outside the library. Every community has local information sources. The ones surveyed here are likely to be found in any city, but every location will also have unique information providers. Be alert for additional possibilities.

Chambers of Commerce and Visitors Bureaus

Promoting their local community is a primary task for chambers of commerce across the nation. Although some have sizable budgets to print promotional materials for visitors and new residents and will send copies on request, many chambers must charge a fee for their publications. Call or write a chamber, explaining your interest, and they will send free materials or a list of those for sale. Get contact information for a chamber in:

World Chamber of Commerce Directory. World Chamber of Commerce Directory. Annual.

This list of chamber of commerce offices throughout the United States provides an address, telephone number, and the name of each chamber manager or president. Also included are addresses and telephone numbers for local convention and visitors' bureaus and economic development organizations.

Every state has an office responsible for promoting tourism within its borders. Like the chambers of commerce, state travel offices publish brochures and promotional literature for visitors. Although most of these publications feature recreational attractions, they also provide a view of what a state has to offer its residents. Many state travel offices provide toll-free telephone numbers for callers. Addresses and telephone numbers may be found in the *World Chamber of Commerce Directory* just described.

Telephone Books

The telephone book is an overlooked source of information about a city. Nearly every community promotes itself in the pages of its telephone book. A special section, often with photographs, illustrations, and maps, highlights newcomer information, special events, local attractions, sports, history, and other items of community interest. If visiting the city, look through this section of the telephone book. Many libraries, by the way, have collections of telephone books from around the nation. Inquire whether the directory for the city you are researching is available in your library.

Local Newspapers

Invest in a subscription to a local newspaper for a month or two. If you are choosing a city based on the recommendations of friends or a city rankings book, reading the local newspaper for a few weeks may be eye-opening, as factors affecting the attractiveness of a city can change quickly. A subscription to the Sunday edition alone is an excellent way to get acquainted with a city. Scanning its pages will help you discern the major issues facing the city in areas such as local government, taxation, the schools, law and order, health services, or employment. Sunday editions often include a weekly calendar of upcoming events in the city—culture, music, sports, and recreation. Classified sections containing the help wanted advertisements and the housing options are also included in the Sunday editions. Remember, too, that nothing else will be as up-to-the-minute as a newspaper. To find the name and address of a local newspaper, try this:

Gale Directory of Publications and Broadcast Media. Gale Research Inc. Annual.

> Arranged by state and city, this guide contains information about newspapers, magazines, and broadcast media in communities throughout the United States. Each newspaper listing provides an address, telephone number, and annual subscription rates, if available. While checking on the newspaper, look at the number and type of broadcast media in the city as well as any magazines published there. Add this nugget of information to the other things you are learning about the city (see Figure 10.5).

Other sources for determining the name and address of a local newspaper are:

Editor and Publisher International Yearbook. Editor & Publisher. Annual.

Working Press of the Nation. National Research Bureau. Annual.

> Both volumes list daily newspapers geographically by state and city. Subscription rates are usually included.

Realtors

A real estate office may be an additional source of information about a new city. In their position as sales agents for residential housing, realtors are familiar with a city's neighborhoods, schools, and community services. Because many real estate offices represent nationally franchised chains, it is possible for a realtor in your hometown to put you in contact with a realtor in the city you are researching. Be sure that the realtor understands how far along you are in deciding to relocate and purchase a new house or apartment. If a move is indefinite, don't expect the realtor to devote a great deal of time to your inquiries.

SUFFOLK† (L7), pop. 47,621.

SE VA. Independent city. On Nansemond River, 17 mi. SW of Portsmouth. Port. Peanut market; meat-packing and tea-processing plants; timber. Manufactures peanut products, bricks, lumber, fertilizer.

30814 Peanut Journal and Nut World
Peanut Journal Publishing Co.
Drawer 347
Suffolk, VA 23434 Phone: (804)484-4804
Magazine on nut farming and marketing. **Founded:** 1921. **Frequency:** Monthly. **Printing Method:** Offset. **Trim Size:** $8^{1}/_{2} \times 11$. **Cols./Page:** 3. **Key Personnel:** Terry Reel, Editor. **ISSN:** 0031-3661. **Subscription:** $25. $3 single issue.
Ad Rates: BW: $400 **Circulation:** (Not Reported)

30815 Suffolk News-Herald
PO Box 1220
Suffolk, VA 23434 Phone: (804)539-3437
General newspaper. **Founded:** June 1873. **Frequency:** Daily (eve.); Sun. (morn.). **Printing Method:** Offset. **Cols./Page:** 6. **Col. Width:** 24 nonpareils. **Col. Depth:** 302 agate lines. **Key Personnel:** Otis T. Amory, Publisher. Earl T. Jones, Jr., Advertising Mgr. **Subscription:** $76; $100 out of area.
Ad Rates: SAU: $6.35 **Circulation:** Daily ★**6,821**
Sun. ★**7,176**
Part of Worrell Enterprises, Inc.

30816 Sun
101 Saratoga St. Phone: (804)934-7550
Suffolk, VA 23434 Fax: (804)934-7515
Local newspaper. **Founded:** 1976. **Frequency:** 3x/wk. (Tues., Thurs., Sun.). **Printing Method:** Offset. **Cols./Page:** 5. **Col. Width:** 26 nonpareils. **Col. Depth:** 182 agate lines. **Key Personnel:** John Pruitt, Editor, Frank Batten, Jr., Publisher, Mike Hevron, Advertising Mgr. **Subscription:** $104.95.
Ad Rates: BW: $553.80 **Circulation:** ‡16,839
4C: $990.80
PCI: $8.52

♣ **30817 WKSV-FM - 96.1**
112 Katherine St.
Suffolk, VA 23452-3723 Phone: (804)431-1550
Format: Religious (Adult Contemporary Christian). **Network(s):** Independent. **Founded:** 1986. **Formerly:** WIAV-FM 1989. **Operating Hours:** 6 a.m.-midnight. **Key Personnel:** Ray Fowler, Gen. Mgr./Program Dir.; Barry Hill, Sales Mgr. **Wattage:** 50,000.

♣ **30818 WLPM-AM - 1450**
444 N. Main St. Phone: (804)539-2394
Suffolk, VA 23434-4425 Fax: (804)539-5130
Format: Oldies. **Network(s):** Satellite Music. **Owner:** Suffolk Broadcasting Co., at above address. **Founded:** 1949. **Operating Hours:** 6 a.m.-10 p.m.; 80% network, 20% local. **Key Personnel:** Sparky Lerner, Client Marketing Consultant. **Wattage:** 1000. **Ad Rates:** $9.50 for 30 seconds; $18 for 60 seconds. **Additional Contact Information:** Mailing Address: PO Box 3019, Suffolk, VA 23434.

Figure 10.5 Typical entry, *Gale Directory of Publications and Broadcast Media*, Volume 1, 124th edition, edited by Julie Winklepleck. Copyright © 1991 by Gale Research Inc. Reproduced by permission.

Local Libraries

Don't forget the public library in the city you are researching. If visiting the city, stop for a quick look at information that can help familiarize you with the city—local guidebooks, issues of the local newspaper and local magazines, local government publications, chamber of commerce brochures, and perhaps more. Many of the publications you find there will only be available locally. The *American Library Directory.* (American Library Association, annual) provides a list of public libraries around the nation with addresses and telephone numbers.

Use Your Imagination

Use your imagination to discover other sources of information about the city you are considering as a new home. Consider where you would go to find out about your present location; then seek similar information sources in the city you are researching. For example, some cities have social organizations for former residents of other states and cities. Find out if there are such groups in your area. Ask family and friends if they know anyone who has lived or visited in the city recently. If you are a college student, ask your admissions office if there are fellow students at your college whose home is in the city you are researching. If the city is a frequent destination for tourists, a travel agent may have brochures describing the area. You may be able to learn your way around a new city long before you relocate.

11 Choosing a Career

Some people grow up knowing what they want to be—a doctor, an engineer, a fireman, a teacher. They make their career choice early, role models are abundant, and they never have doubts or waver from their course. In fact, very few individuals find the choice of a career that simple. More commonly, choosing a career is a process of trial and error, involving tentative appraisals of a variety of options over several years while growing up. Though professional guidance is available from many sources, many would confess to a haphazard approach to reaching a decision. Furthermore, even career choices made with some care and assurance at 18 or 21 may be modified and changed several times over the course of a lifetime. Today, it is not uncommon for an individual to leave one profession for a second, and even a third or fourth, entirely different career field.

Although indecision, chance, and change may always play a role in career choice, you owe it to yourself to make the most of your talents, your skills, and your opportunities. You can do that most successfully by thoroughly investigating career options before you begin to job hunt. You may expand your horizons to encompass careers you did not know existed or realize that you have talents and skills better suited to teaching, for example, than medicine. Once you have information about the entire range of jobs you might enjoy as well as those that best fit your skills and talents—or you know where and how to find this information when you need it—you can seize opportunities for your future wherever and whenever you find them.

BEGIN BY ANALYZING YOUR INTERESTS AND ABILITIES

If you are unsure of your career choice, you must make decisions about the kind of work you would like before you can begin researching employers. For you, the initial step in a job search is to define your career interests. Sit down with a guidance or employment counselor, a trusted friend, or by yourself and make a list of work options you might enjoy.

Define Interests and Preferences

If you are a student, think about the subjects you like or do well in at school or any enjoyable summer and part-time jobs you have had. Consider, too, the activities you enjoy in your spare time. Whether a student or not, evaluate the kind of people-environment you like. Is working alone or in a group more satisfying? Are you a leader or a follower? Is a structured or an unstructured environment more appealing? Third, what kind of tasks appeal to you? Do you like to work with your hands or with your mind? Do you consider yourself machine oriented rather than people oriented? Do you prefer working simultaneously on several multifaceted assignments or on a single integrated project at a time? Finally, think about your personal values and goals. Are independence, responsibility, and decision-making authority important to you? Do you consider a job with impact on people or events, either within a company or outside it, more satisfying? Are status and prestige, whether derived from your career choice, your employer, or a specific job, important to you?

Review Education and Experience

Review the education and experience you have or would need to obtain a job in a chosen field. An academic degree or occupational training is usually the first requirement. In addition, perhaps you have or could acquire a special skill that might enhance your job opportunities, such as foreign language fluency, computer programming skills, or quality control expertise. Internships, seminars, institutes, part-time work, or even student jobs may provide opportunities for gaining experience and skills that you can apply to a career field.

Consider, too, your skills and abilities. For example, do you have artistic ability or creative skills in innovation and experiment? Maybe you enjoy writing or have other communication skills that make editing, teaching, speaking, or selling a satisfying task. Perhaps you are adept at technical or mechanical projects requiring the ability to design, calculate, build, or use your hands or equipment. Analytic or problem-solving skills can be a plus in careers that require the ability to visualize, observe, evaluate, or classify people or activities. A variety of skills in working with people—listening, motivating, negotiating, counseling, teaching, organizing—are in demand in many professions.

Vocational Interest Tests

You may want to take one of the many vocational interest tests available through college placement centers or at employment offices or career counseling services. Such tests allow you to indicate preferences or interests in various subjects, skills, and workplace environments or will measure aptitude for many types of work. When interpreted by a counselor, the completed tests may indicate possible career options. Dozens of such tests are available; a personnel officer or career counselor can suggest the ones most suitable for you.

If you want additional ideas about factors to consider when selecting a career, many books are available. A visit to your local library or bookstore will turn up several to browse through or to take home and study more thoroughly. Ask a librarian or career counselor for recommendations.

FINDING OUT ABOUT CAREERS

After determining the job characteristics that appeal to you and the training and skills you have or must obtain, draw up a list of possible career fields. Now investigate these careers more fully before choosing among them.

Survey Occupational Guides

Every library will list occupational materials, by subject, in its catalog. Some libraries also have pamphlet collections with helpful items. Career materials may include U.S. government publications such as special reports, pamphlets, and statistics. If you are not sure where to begin, ask a librarian for help.

In the library, you will also find guides to occupational information that are excellent starting points for career research. These include:

Occupational Outlook Handbook. U.S. Bureau of Labor Statistics. Biennial.

> This guide covers several hundred occupations, ranging from executive and professional employment to technical and support positions to mechanical and laboring jobs. The description of each occupation includes a discussion of the nature of the work, typical working conditions, training, and other qualifications needed. Current employment levels and job outlook for each career field are surveyed, together with an estimate of average earnings and an evaluation of opportunities for advancement. Sources for obtaining additional information about the occupation are also suggested.

The Encyclopedia of Careers and Vocational Guidance, 8th ed. J.G. Ferguson Publishing Co. 1990.

> This set is similar to the *Occupational Outlook Handbook.* Volume One contains general surveys of 76 industries. The surveys

cover the history and structure of each industry as well as its current outlook. Career paths in the industries are also briefly outlined. Volumes Two, Three, and Four describe several hundred individual occupations. Special features outlined for each occupation in this guide include exceptional as well as general entry-level requirements; suggestions for opportunities to experience or explore a career; and social and psychological factors important to the occupation.

Professional Careers Sourcebook. Gale Research Inc. Biennial.

Providing help in planning careers that require college or technical degrees, this guide lists information sources for careers such as career guides, professional associations, certification agencies, test guides, educational programs, awards and scholarships, and professional and trade publications.

Dictionary of Occupational Titles, 4th ed. rev. U.S. Employment Service. 1991.

This publication does not describe careers or occupations. Rather, it is a list of job titles with brief descriptions of the scope and duties of each job. If you have difficulty defining the kind of job you are interested in or need help imagining the career possibilities that are open to you, this list may be helpful.

In addition to these comprehensive guides, many publishers, including the U.S. government, have books and pamphlets that describe career fields. They often appear in series with titles such as "Careers in . . ." or "So You Want to Be a . . ." Libraries and placement centers often have several such series available. In recent years, a number of guides for career changers have also been published. Ask a librarian or career counselor for suggestions.

As you use published career materials, keep in mind that the information in them may be dated. Check the publication date of any book (usually on the back of the title page); material included may date from as much as two years prior to publication. Both salary levels and the demand for some professions are subject to considerable change over time. Be skeptical, too, of publications that seem to glamorize an occupation or overstate the employment demand and wages. Before making a decision, read several descriptions and seek opinions from additional sources to obtain a variety of perspectives.

Sample a Job

Another way to learn about a career field is by sampling an occupation through an employee exchange, an internship, or (if you are still in school) a summer job. Part-time jobs are another student option. Companies occasionally list such jobs with the college placement center or campus student employment office. College professors may also be aware of opportunities for these jobs. Ask family and friends for suggestions of leads to explore for part-time or summer work. If you are already employed, inquire through your personnel office or ask colleagues and mentors for recommendations. In the library, consult one of the following guides, or an alternative with similar information, for additional opportunities and suggestions:

Internships. Peterson's Guides. Annual.

> This guide lists over 50,000 internship opportunities in 22 broad career areas such as the arts, health services, public interest organizations, industry, and government. Listings are arranged according to the type of company or organization sponsoring the internship. Each listing has descriptive information on the kind and number of positions available in the organization, including salary, if any; eligibility requirements; and application procedure. Includes a geographic index to help those wanting to concentrate internship interests in a certain area. There is also an index of sponsoring organizations.

Summer Employment Directory of the United States. Peterson's Guides. Annual.

> A state-by-state listing of summer jobs, mostly in summer camps, resorts, national parks, restaurants, theme parks, and summer theaters, but also including some jobs in business and industry. This is a good source for anyone wanting experience in hotel, food service, or tourism occupations; also for anyone who wants to work with children and adolescents. Many of the camps listed are for children with special needs.

Directory of Overseas Summer Jobs. Peterson's Guides. Annual.

With 50,000 job listings in over 40 countries, this directory has many suggestions for getting work experience while living and traveling abroad. Especially helpful is the advice about visas, work permits, and health insurance.

Temporary, short-term jobs provide an excellent opportunity to observe what goes on in a representative workplace. You learn what to expect from the day-by-day routine, the typical tasks performed and problems encountered, and the special assignments or opportunities that might arise. You will quickly begin to see whether a particular career is right for you.

Interview a Professional

One more option to explore in learning about a career is to talk to someone already employed in the profession. If you do not know someone you can interview, it may take a bit of ingenuity to locate an appropriate individual. Start by asking colleagues, friends, or teachers for suggestions. Someone at a local newspaper office or the chamber of commerce may be able to suggest the names of likely individuals. Check your newspaper or the yellow pages for firms that employ people in the field you are interested in. Call and ask to speak to the public relations or community affairs representative at the company. Explain your interest and ask if you could schedule an information interview with someone at the firm to learn more about the field you are considering.

If you cannot locate exactly the right person, consider interviewing other people who have an interest in the field and who might be knowledgeable about it. For example, if you are interested in becoming a nutritionist but have difficulty locating a professional to interview, talk to the manager of any large food service operation in a school or hospital. He or she should be able to provide insights into the working conditions and relationships a nutritionist might encounter in that type of setting.

Yet another option is a visit to a local chapter of an appropriate professional association. If you can attend a chapter meeting, you will learn about topics of current interest to professionals in the field. If social time is scheduled before or after the meeting, you will have an opportunity to meet informally with members and ask for their opinions and observations about their career choice.

Prepare carefully for your interviews. Most people enjoy talking about their profession and are flattered to be asked for advice. However, they may resent wasting their time if you have not done your homework before seeing them. Do as much preliminary research on a chosen career field as you can. Make a list of all the questions you would like to have answered and then refine the list down to six or eight really important items. Ask those questions first and then, if time permits, ask about your secondary interests. If possible, interview two or three people about your choice of career fields. Each person will give you his or her own perspective and will have had different experiences.

Investigate Educational Requirements

Once you have decided on a career, you may need additional training or a degree in a special field. Where can you go to get the education you need? The individuals recommended earlier—career counselors, teachers, colleagues, people already in the profession—may be able to advise you and suggest specific programs or training schemes. You can also find answers about further education at the library. Many excellent guides to colleges, describing programs and degrees, the faculty, the student body, and campus life, are available.

If you are seeking a guide to schools offering degrees or training in a particular subject, look at one of the well-known college guides:

Barron's Profiles of American Colleges, 18th ed. Barron's Educational Series, Inc. 1991.

The College Blue Book, 23rd ed. Macmillan. 1991.

Lovejoy's College Guide, 20th ed. Monarch Press. 1991.

> Each of these books has a list or a special volume that identifies specific degree programs or college majors offered at U.S. colleges and universities.

If you are seeking a graduate degree, try this guide:

Peterson's Annual Guides to Graduate Study. Peterson's Guides. Annual.

> Broad descriptions of fields of study include a list of schools offering graduate degrees in the field and notes about entrance requirements, fees, and financial aid available at each school.

If you need additional training in a technical or vocational field, one of these directories may provide an outline of options:

The College Blue Book: Occupational Education, 23rd ed. Macmillan. 1991.

A Directory of Public Vocational-Technical Schools and Institutes in the U.S.A., 5th ed. Media Marketing Group. 1990.

American Trade Schools Directory. Croner Publications. Monthly updates.

Perhaps you need only a short-term program to upgrade your skills, or you want to acquire additional training for a career change. For those purposes, try one of these guides:

Bricker's International Directory. Peterson's Guides. Annual.

> This guide describes about 300 executive education programs for middle and senior level managers offered at colleges and universities in the United States and around the world. Programs range from one week to one year in length. Program descriptions include location, duration, subject matter, costs, and any special features.

Training and Development Organizations Directory, 5th ed. Gale Research Inc. 1991.

> Over 2,500 organizations and the 10,000 workshops, seminars, and training programs they provide to business, industry, and government are described here. Course content, fees, and target audience are noted, where available.

Peterson's Guide to Certificate Programs at American Colleges and Universities. Peterson's Guides. 1988.

This guide covers the specialized certificate programs intended for individuals seeking advancement, relicensure, recertification, and personal growth. Although rather dated, the directory provides a guide to possibilities. Check with the individual school for current program availability.

Many companies provide training after employment. If you already have the academic degree that qualifies you for employment but need special training for the career you seek, consult this volume:

Ray Bard and Susan K. Eliot. *The National Directory of Corporate Training Programs,* 2nd ed. Doubleday. 1988.

This directory, although somewhat dated, lists and describes training programs provided by companies for their employees.

More current information is found in employment guides such as the *CPC Annual* (College Placement Council, annual) or *Dun's Employment Opportunities Directory/The Career Guide* (Dun & Bradstreet Information Service, annual). Both are described in more detail in Chapter 13.

Identify the Factors That Are Important to You

The last step in your preparation for a career choice is to go over your own work values, your personal traits, and your expectations for your job. You will be asked about some of these in employment interviews, and you need to be sure of your own feelings about your future. List the factors that are most important to you and refer to them as you write your cover letter, assemble a resume, and prepare for your interviews. It may also be helpful to review the list as you evaluate a prospective employer and, later on, consider job offers. Enjoy your research—it will be invaluable in locating the perfect job for you.

12 Researching the "Extra Mile"

Do you still want to learn more details about a prospective employer? Maybe you have a few questions whose answers you haven't been able to locate and feel your evaluation is incomplete without resolving those issues. Remember, some questions will always go unanswered. The facts you want to locate may not be published in an easily accessible source, and your personal contacts may not be able to help. The company research suggestions in Part II, which survey the most useful and widely available information sources, will answer many questions about large companies and provide direction for creative approaches to small company research. However, additional information options do exist. If you have become a determined fact finder while doing preliminary research on a prospective employer, here are more avenues to explore.

ELECTRONIC BUSINESS INFORMATION SOURCES

Electronic information sources play a valuable and growing role in providing business information. They comprise several types of materials; those most commonly available are online databases and compact discs.

Online Databases

Online databases are information files or records stored on computer tape. Access is possible through software developed by the database vendor who houses the tapes. A telecommunications network provides the link between the vendor's tapes and a user's microcomputer or terminal. By searching in the files for specific words or concepts, often linking them together logically, a user can retrieve from the thousands of database records precisely those items related to his or her need. Such a search may take only a few minutes and the results can be accurate and highly specific.

The speed and power of electronic systems are valuable for any research. Information in database files is often highly specialized and available in no other form. Many files are updated on a daily basis. But despite the exceptional research value, there are drawbacks. Few systems are global—no group of databases covers the entire universe of knowledge. Though pertinent material is identified, the full text may not be available. Business databases are among the most expensive offered, and cost can be prohibitive if search fees are charged to the researcher. Nevertheless, online databases provide versatile and powerful access to information.

Compact Discs

Databases may also be stored on compact discs; these products can be made directly available on a microcomputer equipped to read a compact disc. The compact discs are often referred to as CD-ROM (compact disc-read only memory) products. They provide the same precise and rapid access to information as online databases. They also have many of the same drawbacks. Although most compact disc products are user friendly, software is not standardized. While updates are usually monthly, some are less frequent.

Access to Electronic Sources

In most libraries, a librarian will help you select an online database to search for information on your subject and will perform the search for you. Because the software used to access the databases is somewhat complex, a librarian trained as an online searcher can perform the search more rapidly and precisely. Some libraries have "end-user" programs where you can learn to do your own searches. Usually you must pay a fee for the service that can vary depending on the database and the amount of computer connect time used.

Some vendors offer direct database access to individual users like you. By setting up a payment account with the vendor and getting a password to access the system, you may do online information searches at home or in your office. The systems are menu driven and user friendly. Your costs may be less as an individual user than at a library, if you use the systems in off-peak hours. Both Dialog Information Services and BRS Information Technologies, the online vendors commonly found in libraries, offer a user-friendly version of their database systems to the nonspecialist. Additional vendors offering database systems to the nonspecialist user are CompuServe, Dow Jones News/Retrieval, Mead Data Central, and NewsNet. Addresses and telephone numbers of these vendors, as well as brief descriptions of the databases they offer, can be found at your library.

With a few minutes of instruction, anyone can use most compact disc products. Currently only a few CD-ROM information products are sold directly to individuals; most are found in libraries and offices. CD-ROM products are often networked in libraries, providing simultaneous access to several users. There is generally no fee for using compact disc products, although some libraries may charge for paper and printing.

Content of Electronic Sources

A broad spectrum of business and financial data is available in both electronic formats. Some database files are bibliographic, referring users to information in other publications. In addition to indexing of periodicals and other documents, bibliographic databases may also have abstracts or summaries of the publications cited. A second group of databases are "full text," providing the complete text of documents. A third type are factual, providing statistics, financial data, or directory information. For job-hunting purposes, all three of these types may be useful.

Many of the information sources mentioned in Part II are available in electronic format. Business directories are one example. The periodical indexes and some financial documents suggested for your use are also accessible electronically. Availability of specific items in these formats has been noted throughout Part II. In addition to the electronic sources previously noted, hundreds of additional databases are available, many of them with information valuable for business research.

To give you an idea of the variety and scope of information available in electronic form, here's a brief sample beginning with directory files that often contain records for several million companies.

American Business Directory. American Business Information. Quarterly updates.

> This database includes directory, financial, and market share information for nearly seven million U.S. firms in all product and industry areas. Branch locations, subsidiaries, and divisions can be easily identified, as well as many small, private firms.

Teikoku Databank. Teikoku Databank. Quarterly updates.

> An example of a directory file with extensive data for foreign firms, this online file covers 45,000 Japanese companies that conduct business overseas.

Other electronic sources provide specialized information not widely accessible elsewhere. Look at these examples:

PTS New Product Announcements/Plus. Predicasts. Weekly updates.

> This online database provides the full text of press releases and company announcements about new technologies, products, and services. It may be useful in tracking market strategies or a company's R&D activity.

Business Dateline. UMI/Data Courier. Weekly updates.

> Providing easy access to the full text of hundreds of regional business publications and the news releases of several thousand

organizations, this database profiles the activities of companies of all sizes, large and small. The detail found here seldom appears in more widely distributed national publications.

Corporate financial information is available in a number of online databases. The financial disclosure reports filed with the U.S. Securities and Exchange Commission (SEC) are available in full or partial form in several files. Other databases with financial information include the following:

Insider Trading Monitor. Invest/Net Group Inc. Daily updates.

Stock trades by officers and directors of publicly owned corporations are tracked by this online file. Such data is valuable in measuring the volatility of a company's financial position.

M&A Filings. Charles E. Simon & Co. Daily updates.

The details of corporate merger and acquisition documents filed with the SEC and contained in this online database may include financial data not easily accessible elsewhere.

Several databases cover specific industries such as biotechnology, electronics, food, and pharmaceuticals. Trademarks and patents can be tracked in others. Newswire services available as databases provide daily updates of news releases from around the world. Many facets of corporate activity can be explored using electronic access. Details of the content and coverage of online files, their availability, and cost are available at your library or directly from a database supplier or vendor.

Just like online databases, compact disc products have developed greater variety and content as they have become more numerous and more widely available. For example, the proliferation of compact disc products has seen the introduction of several comprehensive electronic resources for business. In a single datafile, they may include both directory and financial information for a large number of companies, plus indexing of periodical articles about the firms. The advantage of such products is the gathering together of pertinent corporate information in one easy-to-use source with electronic access allowing quick, highly specific retrieval of desired items. Two of the best-known comprehensive compact disc resources for business are:

General Business File. Information Access Co.

Lotus One Source/Corporate. Lotus Development Corporation. Monthly updates.

> Both contain information on several thousand corporations from a variety of sources. Expect to find both directory information and financial and investment data as well as biographical information about top executives and citations to relevant periodical articles.

These are both very expensive products and are likely to be accessible in only the largest libraries. Remember, however, that the information in these comprehensive compact disc files is also available in a number of alternative sources, both print and electronic. It may take longer to put the information together if you must search in several places, but the result should be the same as using a comprehensive electronic product.

GUIDES TO BUSINESS RESEARCH

In general, the preceding chapters discuss only widely available sources of company information. Many other specialized materials exist. The easiest way to find out about additional research options is to ask a librarian for suggestions. However, you may want to try your own hand at tracking down resources. Business research is not difficult if you are willing to spend time learning about the available options. Of the several available guides to business research, some are meant for librarians and professional researchers; others are for people like you who want to learn to do their own research. Here are a few examples, starting with those often used by librarians to learn about business information materials.

Lorna M. Daniells. *Business Information Sources.* University of California Press. 1985.

> Long a classic in the field and well known to business librarians, this guide is intended for the librarian, the business student, and the businessperson. It includes not only descriptions

of reference sources, but also books and texts in several business subfields.

Diane Wheeler Strauss. *Handbook of Business Information.* Libraries Unlimited. 1988.

Also intended for students and researchers as well as librarians, this guide identifies and describes business reference sources with illustrations of how they are used. It also explains many basic business concepts for the inexperienced user.

Michael R. Lavin. *Business Information: How to Find It, How to Use It,* 2nd ed. Oryx Press. 1992.

Intended for both experienced researchers and novices, each chapter begins with an explanation of business concepts necessary to understand the materials introduced. This is not a comprehensive guide, but one focusing on the most widely available and well-respected business research materials.

As an introduction to a broad range of business reference materials, any of the preceding guides are excellent. All are easy to understand and can provide guidance for library research in all fields of business. If you want to focus on information sources for specific industries or on career and employment information for specific occupations, here are two additional guides to sample for suggestions:

Job Hunters Sourcebook. Gale Research Inc. 1991.

Encyclopedia of Business Information Sources, 8th ed. Gale Research Inc. 1990.

Both of these guides list potential information sources under either a specific career or an industry. For example, career fields listed in the first volume are subdivided into categories such as manuals, directories, employment agencies, placement services, and trade journals with job ads. The second volume lists handbooks, trade associations, periodicals, directories, statistics sources, financial ratios, and online databases for each industry covered. Use either of these guides to help identify the specialized information sources of a specific career field or an industry.

Perhaps you want to go beyond the library and its materials. You may be seeking unusual research possibilities, options for identifying sources of information that only the diligent researcher might uncover. Because these unusual sources can occasionally yield big payoffs in information difficult to obtain elsewhere, they are sometimes well worth the time and effort to pursue. Don't forget, however, that even lengthy and exhaustive research can also lead to inconclusive results and dead ends.

Two guides to creative and unorthodox information leads that also include more conventional resources are the following:

Leonard M. Fuld. *Competitor Intelligence.* John Wiley & Sons. 1985.

> An interesting and informative guide to both traditional and creative information sources useful for tracking data about companies and their competitive positions, this volume surveys both library materials and those found elsewhere. Written by a seasoned practitioner in the field, the most compelling chapters deal with unconventional techniques and resources that the intelligent professional or amateur can employ when seeking information about any company, big or small.

How to Find Information about Companies: The Corporate Intelligence Source Book, 7th ed. Washington Researchers Publishing. 1989.

> This do-it-yourself guide for company researchers was prepared by a professional information-gathering firm. It provides tips and suggestions for using printed materials and library resources, state and national government agencies, company and industry experts, and professional information and investigation services.

HIRING A PROFESSIONAL RESEARCHER

If the thought of research has you spinning or you simply don't have time to undertake company research yourself, perhaps you should consider hiring a professional researcher. Over the past decade, the number and variety of firms offering such services have grown rapidly. Some are large nationally known research bureaus; others are fee-based services offered through academic or nonprofit institutions; still others are small independent information brokers. Although a few specialize in employment research, working for executive recruiters, career services, or personnel departments, most provide a variety of services to a broad based clientele.

A professional researcher specializing in employment services can quickly produce a list of target companies for you to consider, based on your interests and qualifications, and can investigate the firms for the factors you want to know. Using resources such as those described in this book, as well as other specialized electronic and print sources, the information the researcher provides will be as current, thorough, and accurate as the available data allows. Some researchers will also provide additional services—supplying copies of relevant documents, ranking companies according to selected criteria, or mailing resumes.

You can identify a research firm or professional in several ways. One of the easiest is to consult a directory. Try one of these:

Helen Burwell. *Directory of Fee Based Information Services.* Burwell Enterprises. 1990.

The FISCAL Directory of Fee-Based Information Services in Libraries. FYI/County of Los Angeles Public Library. Biennial.

> Both of these directories list firms and agencies providing document retrieval, subject specialists, database searchers, information brokers, and others around the nation providing library and information services. The services offered by each are briefly noted.

Alternatively you might ask for referrals from a career placement or executive recruitment firm. Some libraries can provide the names of information brokers in their area. Before hiring, check to ensure that any firm you consider is reputable. Ask for the names of previous clients and contact them about their satisfaction with the service. Ask about the information resources used by the firm and get a fee schedule or cost estimate.

Fees for professional research services can be high, beginning at a minimum of $50/hour plus additional costs for electronic searches, document retrieval, and other extras such as full background information on firms and copies of supporting documents. Expect to pay more for any special requests or requirements you may have.

Don't forget that you can, of course, do the research yourself for much less. Nearly all the sources used by a professional are also available to you as outlined throughout this book. Your chief expenditure will be your time. If you use the suggestions from previous chapters, review the guides to business research in this chapter, and ask for advice and assistance from librarians and information specialists as you work, you will be well prepared to succeed in your company research.

PART IV

USING COMPANY INFORMATION IN A JOB SEARCH

13 Identifying Prospective Employers

Checking employment ads in a newspaper, visiting an employment or placement office, or calling a network of personal contacts may be your first impulse as you begin to job hunt. Look at companies and organizations that already employ people with your training and skills, but don't forget that opportunities may also exist in less obvious locations. Not all accountants, for example, work for accounting firms or the accounting departments of government and industry. Museums, theaters, amusement parks, public interest groups, charitable foundations, and many other organizations also need accountants. Interesting, satisfying jobs can be found in many places.

WHAT PUBLISHED RESOURCES CAN HELP TO IDENTIFY EMPLOYERS?

Begin a job search with firms that have suitable openings, or alternatively, identify companies of interest to you and pursue opportunities with them. Either approach will work; in a job-scarce environment, a combination of both may improve your chances.

Just as company research can begin in the library and move on to sources outside it, use the same technique to identify employment opportunities. Look first at easily accessible material in the library, studying it thoroughly for background and leads. With this framework in place, you can take full advantage of additional information elsewhere. Let's look first at sources that identify organizations already employing people with your skills or background and then at ways to identify position vacancies.

Business Directories

If you want to work in a particular industry or with a firm that produces a specific product or service, begin by checking company directories. Most have an index by product or industry. Use that index to draw up an initial list of companies to research. Each chapter of Part II has suggestions of business directories you can use. The best-known directories, the *Million Dollar Directory* (Dun & Bradstreet Information Services, annual), *Standard & Poor's Register of Corporations, Directors, and Executives* (Standard & Poor's Corp., annual), and *Ward's Business Directory of U.S. Private and Public Companies* (Gale Research Inc., annual), all have industry indexes. *Thomas Register of American Manufacturers* (Thomas Publishing Co., annual) has a detailed product listing that identifies manufacturers engaged with a particular product. All of these directories are fully described in Chapter 4. Since dozens of companies are listed under a single industry or product, think about additional criteria, such as location or size, that you might apply to draw up a manageable list of potential employers.

Don't overlook state industrial directories when searching for employers. These include many smaller companies as well as branch locations of the corporations listed in national business directories. If you are concentrating on a specific location in a job search, the state directories may be especially useful.

Trade directories that cover a single industry can also identify a group of possible employers. Some of these directories list not only manufacturers, but also their suppliers and distributors. To determine the trade directories for an industry, look for this volume in your library: *Directories in Print* (Gale Research Inc., annual). This guide, described more fully in Chapter 4, can help you identify relevant directories.

Once you have a directory title, see if it is available in your library. If not, *Directories in Print* gives purchase information. Alternatively, ask a librarian to suggest a directory that might be available. Also, some trade directories are published as special issues of an industry trade journal. A librarian can help you determine if this is the case for the industry you are considering.

Employment Directories

Another type of directory to consult for suggestions is an employment directory. These guides list and describe companies in certain employment categories. They may be most useful if you are seeking an entry-level position or are changing careers. Among the most familiar of the employment directories are these:

CPC Annual. College Placement Council. Annual.

> The major part of this directory, Volumes 2–4, consists of company profiles. Each profile has a brief description of the company, its general employment opportunities, employee benefits, and an address to contact for further information. Volume 2 covers employers in business, administrative, and nontechnical areas; Volume 3 has scientific and engineering positions; and Volume 4 surveys the health sciences. Indexes lead to specific occupations, geographical locations, or employers.

Dun's Employment Opportunities Directory/The Career Guide. Dun & Bradstreet Information Services. Annual.

> This directory also details employment opportunities and hiring practices of major U.S. companies. About 5,000 companies are profiled with descriptions of their general employment needs, educational requirements, and company benefits. A special feature is a state-by-state list of professional personnel consultants and their specialities.

The National Job Bank. Bob Adams Inc. Annual.

> Arranged by state, this directory briefly describes companies with, where available, a list of occupational fields commonly employed, educational background sought, and company benefits provided. Indexes are by industry and city.

Peterson's Business and Management Jobs. Peterson's Guides. Annual.

Peterson's Engineering, Science and Computer Jobs. Peterson's Guides. Annual.

> Each provides the following information about the firms listed: a company description, entry level position profiles, starting salaries, training opportunities, fringe benefits, and types of degrees sought. Special features such as internships and international opportunities are noted.

General business directories don't usually list a firm's personnel officer. The preceding employment directories give the address of the personnel office, but often no name. Many career advisors suggest that a letter of application always be addressed to the personnel officer by name. To trace that individual, look for this directory:

CPC National Directory. College Placement Council. Annual.

> The subtitle of this directory is "Who's Who in Career Planning, Placement and Recruitment." The first half lists college placement directors; the second half, the names of personnel officers for major companies. If companies have several locations, the personnel officer for each location may be listed. Some government agencies and service organizations are also included.

Another possibility is to call the company you are considering and ask the receptionist for the personnel officer's name (and the correct spelling). You will rarely be refused this information.

If you are seeking a management position and want to contact an executive search firm to do your job hunting for you, directories of these professionals are also available. Here's one example:

The Directory of Executive Recruiters. Kennedy Publications. Annual.

> This book describes over 2,000 firms that are executive "headhunters"—businesses that seek the right managers for top

corporate positions. All firms listed are members of the Association of Executive Search Consultants and are only those compensated by management, not by you, for their services. Indexes by industry, function, and geographic area locate those firms best suited to your needs.

By the way, if you want clues as to how the executive search process is carried out, look at this book:

Andrea A. Jupina. *The Handbook of Executive Search Research.* Kennedy Publications. 1992.

Essentially a how-to manual for corporate recruiters, this book can provide insights on how professionals identify potential candidates for management positions. It also reinforces the value of good background research in a library prior to client contacts.

Company Profiles

Many popular books that briefly profile major national corporations may help you choose an initial list of companies to review. All look at companies that are tops in their field, interesting, successful, or good places to work. Some of the studies are rather dated, but all are starting points for identifying characteristics of a good employer. If you choose a list of possible employers based on these authors' recommendations, be sure to supplement the descriptions with recent information. Representative titles include:

William J. Birnes and Gary Markman. *Selling at the Top: The 100 Best Companies in America to Sell For.* Harper & Row. 1985.

Robert Levering, Milton Moskowitz, and Michael Katz. *The 100 Best Companies to Work for in America.* Addison-Wesley. 1984.

Michael D. Harkavy and the Philip Lief Group. *The 100 Best Companies to Sell For.* John Wiley & Sons. 1989.

Hal Morgan and Kerry Tucker. *Companies That Care.* Simon and Schuster. 1991.

Milton Moskowitz, Robert Levering, and Michael Katz. *Everybody's Business: A Field Guide to the 400 Leading Companies in America.* Doubleday. 1990.

Milton Moskowitz. *The Global Marketplace: 102 of the Most Influential Companies outside America.* Macmillan. 1987.

Jack Plunkett. *The Almanac of American Employers: A Guide to America's 500 Most Successful Large Corporations.* Contemporary Books. 1985.

Baila Zeitz and Lorraine Dusky. *The Best Companies for Women.* Simon and Schuster. 1988.

Ron Zemke with Dick Schaaf. *The Service Edge: 101 Companies That Profit from Customer Care.* New American Library. 1989.

Periodicals and Newspapers

Periodicals and newspapers provide good job search opportunities, both to identify possible employers and to learn about positions currently available. To identify employers, for example, start by reading recent issues of several periodicals. Sample national business periodicals such as *Business Week, Fortune Magazine,* or *Forbes;* or read *The Wall Street Journal* for several weeks. All of these contain articles about individual companies and industries, often those embarking on new ventures, having marked successes, or preparing expansion plans. Your reading will also provide a taste of current issues facing American business and industry and a view of the nation's economic outlook.

If you know the industry you want to work in, read the trade and professional journals in the field. These will directly address the issues you need to be familiar with in the industry. And, because these periodicals frequently highlight top companies and their managers, you not only learn who's who in the industry but why they are the leaders. You become aware of the standard for excellence in the industry and can measure a potential employer by the factors you have learned are important. Your reading will also provide insights into the job market in your field.

If you want a job near your hometown or another specific locality, read the business section of the local newspaper. If there are regional business journals, and there generally are in most states and major metropolitan areas, browse through several issues. Like the national publications, these will outline local economic and employment conditions. Companies will be profiled in the pages of these publications, expansion plans outlined, new processes and products highlighted, promotions and retirements noted.

If you want to relocate and your library doesn't carry a newspaper for the area, invest in a few months' subscription for yourself. The price will be low for the value the newspaper provides in locating a job in the city you have chosen. Find the name and address of newspapers in one of the following:

Gale Directory of Publications and Broadcast Media. Gale Research Inc. Annual.

Editor and Publisher International Yearbook. Editor & Publisher. Annual.

Working Press of the Nation. National Research Bureau. Annual.

See more about these directories in Chapter 10.

Everyone associates newspapers with job advertisements. Read them carefully if you are seeking currently available positions. Sunday editions carry the majority of advertisements each week. Newspapers in major metropolitan areas often carry job advertisements from across the nation, but many companies concentrate newspaper advertisements within the geographical region where the position is available.

If your access to newspapers is limited, look for one of these alternatives:

National Business Employment Weekly. Dow Jones & Co. Weekly.

> This weekly newspaper reprints the block ads from the daily regional editions of *The Wall Street Journal.* Most are business and management positions. Also included are articles on general job search techniques. This publication is widely available at newsstands and employment services.

National Ad Search. National Ad Search. Weekly.

> This newspaper reprints the large help wanted advertisements from several major daily newspapers across the country. Most positions included are managerial, technical, and professional. Because it is based on reprints, job ads will be posted here somewhat later than they originally appeared.

Newspapers are not the only publications to carry job advertisements. Trade and professional journals and newsletters also have them. Many firms prefer to advertise in these publications because they have wide readership among people in the field, those most likely to be job candidates. In addition, the geographic scope of these publications, whether national, regional, or local, may also be exactly what the company seeks in its job candidates. In other words, this is target advertising aimed to reach the greatest number of potential candidates.

To identify the trade and professional journals for your field, try one of these directories:

Ulrich's International Periodicals Directory. R. R. Bowker. Annual.

The Standard Periodical Directory. Oxbridge Communications, Inc. Annual.

Gale Directory of Publications and Broadcast Media. Gale Research Inc. Annual.

> All of these directories have a subject index or list of trade journals by field to help in identifying those for a specific industry. From the descriptions you can usually determine if a journal accepts advertising, although not employment ads specifically.

Because only selected journals carry job advertisements, you may need to scan several to locate those that do. A timesaver for this step is:

S. Norman Feingold and Glenda Ann Hansard-Winkler. *Where the Jobs Are: A Comprehensive Directory of 1200 Journals Listing Career Opportunities.* Garrett Park Press. 1989.

Discover quickly the journals that carry job listings for your field. An index by careers directs you to the journals most likely to be relevant.

If this directory is not available, ask someone already in the field, or familiar with it, to identify the periodicals that are the best employment sources. If you are a college student, ask a faculty advisor or placement center staff.

Electronic Business Information Sources

A search of either an online database or a compact disc product provides quick, highly specific retrieval of information about companies and industries. A search is also an option to consider when compiling a list of possible employers. In a matter of minutes, you can obtain a list of companies, fitting your personal criteria, to contact about employment.

Assume, for example, that you want to work for a national corporation and that your library has access to online databases (or maybe you have access on your home computer). The librarian who helps you prepare for an online search will suggest that you be specific about your interests. Otherwise your list will include hundreds of companies and the cost of your search may be very high. For a manageable list you might opt to look only at companies of a certain size, maybe 500 employees or more, in a specific industry, perhaps food processing. Should this profile still produce a list of more than 50 companies, limit your choices to those located in only three or four states or those in a specific branch of the industry such as candy making. Your goal is a list of 10 to 12 companies to research in more depth. You can always return for a second search, for additional company names or a different industry. If fees are charged for the computer search, you also want to keep within your budget.

Compact disc products provide the same fast, specific retrieval of information. If your library has a compact disc product with company information, you can do an employer identification search yourself, often at little or no cost. Again, be specific about the kind of companies you are interested in. Start by searching broadly for a characteristic important to you—

maybe any company headquartered in California. Then choose one or two industries and perhaps any company with annual sales over $50 million. In a few minutes, you will have a list of companies to research and, perhaps, contact about employment. In addition to names and addresses, either electronic format can also provide additional information about the firms on your list.

While electronic sources are quick, straightforward ways to gather employer leads, they do have some drawbacks. Databases only list or describe companies; they do not indicate a company's employment needs or whether positions in your field are currently available. Although companies of all types and sizes may be included, many databases concentrate only on large public corporations, omitting small or privately owned companies that may be excellent employers. If a library charges a fee for electronic information access, get a cost estimate before you start. Despite the speed and ease of this option, costs escalate quickly for complex or lengthy searches. Remember that most, although not all, of the information found in electronic sources can also be found in published resources. If time is not a factor, print alternatives may serve you adequately.

WHAT'S AVAILABLE OUTSIDE THE LIBRARY?

The library is only a first stop in putting together a list of possible employers and current job openings. There are several other sources of information. You will probably think of others in addition to the ones suggested here.

College Placement Centers

If you are a college student, get acquainted with the services and resources of the placement center. This office maintains listings of current job openings, both nationally and locally. Many companies visit campuses each year to discuss their firm's employment opportunities for upcoming graduates. The placement center assists in scheduling interviews with the companies' representatives during their campus visit.

Recruitment materials provided by companies are also available in the placement center. Browse through this material for ideas about firms to research as well as for clues to the kind of employee sought. If you find a match between a need for your skills and an interesting, successful company, you have identified a firm to research in more depth and, perhaps, to contact about job openings.

Professional Associations

Professional associations are excellent sources of employment information. To identify an association in your field, ask for this guide at your library.

Encyclopedia of Associations. Gale Research Inc. Annual.

> This is a comprehensive listing of all types of associations, including those of professional groups. A keyword index helps to identify the appropriate ones for your career field.

With the association name, you hold a key to information and jobs. If you are a college student, become a student member. This is a good way to learn more about a career and job opportunities. Also, membership looks good on your resume. Student membership rates are generally low and you receive most of the benefits of full membership. Often a student chapter will meet jointly with a local professional chapter. Here you can meet professionals already working in your field who may know of job openings and be familiar with companies you are interested in. Take advantage of such meetings to form a personal information and mentoring network.

If you are a working professional looking for a new job, the professional association also has much to offer you. You get the same benefits that are important to a student member: opportunities to meet others in the field, a knowledge of major employers, a network of colleagues, and perhaps early notice of job openings. In addition to local chapter contacts and meetings, you may attend national association meetings and establish a wider network of colleagues with similar interests and background. The opportunity to establish mentor relationships with senior colleagues is a primary benefit.

Over and above these personal contacts, membership usually includes copies of association publications. Most groups publish a newsletter or journal and a common feature of these publications is a list of current job openings. Some associations also have a job hot line, an 800 number to call for current job openings.

Employment Agencies and Programs

Every state offers an employment program to assist job seekers. The services and opportunities vary from state to state, but most have offices in major cities and each county. Many companies list their vacancies with the state agency and the positions available range from clerical and mechanical jobs to technical and professional opportunities. Civil service positions with the state or local government are also likely to be listed here. Counselors in these offices are often familiar with local employers and may be able to suggest companies to consider, even if openings are not presently listed.

Employment programs and counseling offered under government auspices are a special option for women and minorities. These programs make an effort to gather information about prospective employers and job openings that may not be widely available elsewhere.

Private employment agencies and executive recruitment services may be most useful if you have specialized training or considerable professional experience. Even if you are seeking only an entry-level position, most agency counselors will be happy to discuss employment possibilities and to accept a copy of your resume for their files. Agencies generally charge a fee for their services if they find employment for you. In some instances the fee may be paid by the employer who hires you, but in others you may be expected to pay. Before signing any contract with an agency, ascertain who will pay, how much, and when the payment is due.

Personal Networks

Don't overlook your personal contacts. Almost everyone in the course of their work, reading or talking with others, gathers information and forms opinions about companies and job opportunities. Thus, family, teachers, friends, colleagues, and current and past employers may all have suggestions for you. They may know of people moving on or retiring, who have created a job opening with a company that may be exactly right for you. They may hear rumors of expansion or new companies moving into the area. In some instances, they may have access to published materials of restricted circulation that contain information about industries, companies, or available positions.

You may think that you do not know anyone who could help you in this way. Ask yourself who also has an interest in your career field or the company and industry that you want to work in. Who needs to know, or who can tell you who needs to know, about your field or the industry? If you analyze the question in those terms you may think of several individuals or offices that can help. Also, ask the people who assist you for suggestions of others to contact. Both librarians and career counselors, for example, have good ideas and lots of experience in helping people track down company information and job opportunities. Few individuals will fail to be flattered if you ask for their advice and opinions about career options. Developing a network of contacts is an ongoing process and you never know when or from whom you will hear about the perfect job or the perfect employer.

14 Using Your Research in Resumes, Cover Letters, and Interviews

The final step in researching a prospective employer is putting your knowledge of a company to work for you. By now you have made a list of companies that are your initial choices as possible employers. Your education and experience match the companies' needs. You have looked at the size, financial status, current management practices, long-term industry outlook, and employee programs for each company in as much depth as available resources and time allowed. Based on your research, you are confident that these companies have the characteristics that you want in an employer. You are ready to inquire about employment opportunities.

Alternatively, you may have reached this final step by locating actual job openings. You, too, have done your research and have chosen the positions you are most interested in, based on what you have learned about the companies and your preferences. You are also ready to make your initial contact with the prospective employers.

Many books offer advice about preparing your resume and cover letter. Periodicals and newspapers also regularly feature articles that discuss this aspect of a job search. Scan several sources to get an idea of what to include and how to package this important information. Career counselors, colleagues, and friends may also have useful tips. Because this kind of information is so widely available, it will not be discussed here—except for the role to be played by the company research you have just completed.

THE RESUME

A resume focuses on you; it describes your education, experience, and accomplishments. How can you apply company research to your resume? The answer is: indirectly, in the items you choose to include or emphasize about yourself. Perhaps your previous work experience is in the same industry as that of the companies you have chosen. Maybe you possess a special skill or ability that is in demand. Possibly a company offers experience in a field that would allow you to advance in your career. Several scenarios for highlighting the interplay between your qualifications and a company's current position are possible. Let's look briefly at two examples of resumes using company research.

Sample Resume for Janet Logan

Janet Logan is a recent accounting graduate. Her long-term goal is a management position with an international corporation; she is particularly hoping for an opportunity to work abroad. Janet has spent time researching potential employers and is especially interested in a group of companies that are subsidiaries of foreign-owned corporations. Janet wants her resume to stand out from the hundreds of others these companies will receive, but her grades were only slightly above average and in recent summers she has worked as a lifeguard. However, she has been recognized for her efforts in organizing a student chapter of the Association of Accountants on her campus and serving as its first president. One of her accomplishments as president was to organize a volunteer income tax advisory service for other students. She has also been an active and sought-after participant in local community events. As a teenager, Janet lived in France for two years and she spent a summer studying and traveling in Spain. These experiences have contributed to her foreign language skills.

For the position she hopes to obtain, Janet Logan has two items she should emphasize in her resume—her language ability and her skills as an organizer and leader among her peers. Although neither her grade point average or work experience are out of the ordinary, her resume can reveal that she has initiative and the ability to lead others and that she has interest and experience in living outside the United States.

On a visit to her campus placement office, Janet learned of an entry-level opening in the financial division of one of the multinational firms she is interested in. Not only is this division located just a few hours from her hometown, but when researching the firm, she discovered that it is widely known for its outstanding management training program. Best of all, the program often includes an opportunity for qualified employees to gain experience in one of the firm's international divisions located in Europe. Figure 14.1 shows the resume Janet Logan will be sending to the company.

Janet has clearly outlined the type of position and employer she seeks in her statement of career objective. The position offered by Woodford/Metier International, the firm that has a trainee position available, fits this profile. Her major fields of study fit the position requirements, and Janet has noted her language skills. Her role in establishing the Association of Accountants chapter and the student tax service on her campus, in addition to increasingly responsible volunteer positions in a local community event, are clearly evident. Janet's resume emphasizes her skills while demonstrating how she meets the qualifications sought by the company for entry-level positions. The resume is keyed to a specific firm and the opportunities it offers.

Look also at this example of a job hunter with several years' experience who is searching for a managerial position.

Sample Resume for Frank Stone

Frank Stone has been employed for the past 12 years by a firm that manufactures brick, first as a Project Engineer, then Chief

Janet E. Logan
2333 Maple Street
Oakdale, Illinois 58677
(325-555-4161)

CAREER OBJECTIVE

Financial accounting position with international corporation offering opportunity for management training.

EDUCATION

B.A. in Accounting 1992; concentration on financial accounting and accounting information systems Oakdale University, Oakdale, Illinois

Summer Semester in Spain, Certificate 1991; courses in international management and Spanish language Universidad de Merida, Merida, Spain

HONORS AND AWARDS

Dean's Award for service to College of Business Administration 1991; selected on basis of service to college and promise for achievement in career field

Selected as resident, Maison Francais, 1991/92, residence hall for advanced students of French language

ACCOMPLISHMENTS, ACTIVITIES, AND SKILLS

Organized student chapter of the Association of Accountants at Oakdale University, 1991; President of chapter, 1991/92

Organized and coordinated free income tax advisory service offered by 30 volunteer advanced accounting students to 12,000 member student body of Oakdale University in April 1991 and 1992

Participant, 1988-92, Oakdale Festival of Nations Community Fair; Chairman, French Booth, 1991; Member of Festival Steering Committee, 1992

Fluency in spoken and written French, good skills in spoken Spanish, limited knowledge of Portuguese; extensive travel in Europe in addition to 2 years' residence in France and 4 months' residence in Spain

Tutor to first-year French language students 1990-92

WORK EXPERIENCE

Lifeguard, Oakdale Community Swimming Club, summers, 1986-90, earned 50% of college tuition costs

Figure 14.1 Resume of Janet Logan.

of Project Engineering, and now as Plant Facilities Manager. He has special strengths in managing people and was responsible for introducing an innovative team approach to the Project Engineering division that proved highly successful and was later expanded to all production units within the company. He is also knowledgeable about high-temperature furnaces and the special handling needs of powder materials and hopes to remain in an industry utilizing these skills. His current career goal is a position as Plant Manager with full responsibility for a manufacturing facility.

Frank Stone, like Janet Logan, will emphasize his particular strengths in his resume, most notably his ability to successfully organize, motivate, and manage people. He also has knowledge of a specialized industry dealing with raw materials in powder form and with high-temperature production methods. Since he hopes to remain in this industry, he has been in touch with several personal contacts in firms across the nation. From a professional colleague, he has learned of an opening in a nearby state. A company has a new factory to manufacture ceramic tile under construction and is seeking a plant manager. After researching the firm and finding it a leader in its niche of the industry, with a good record on innovation, quality, and financial strength, Frank Stone prepared the resume shown in Figure 14.2 to submit with his application for that position.

Frank Stone's resume, while outlining his duties in a series of increasingly responsible positions, highlights his special skills and accomplishments. His background clearly meets the requirements of the company and shows that he has successful experience in introducing quality control programs and innovative management procedures. He knows from his research that these skills are of vital interest to the new company. The resume should be considered very favorably by Deco-Tile.

THE COVER LETTER

A good cover letter is an important part of the job-seeking process. A well-written and well-constructed cover letter not only will highlight your qualifications and experience but will also make your application stand out from others with similar experience.

Frank L. Stone
3220 Walnut Street
Kirkland, Missouri 62111
(314-555-6781)

SUMMARY:

Professional engineer with 12 years of progressive management experience in the brick industry. Full responsibility for supervision of over 30 engineers and technicians. Strong record in cost control, quality assurance, and innovative work team organization.

WORK HISTORY:

Patriot Brick Inc., 1800 Foundry Road, Kirkland, Missouri

Patriot Brick manufactures ceramic brick for the construction industry, has annual sales of $30 million, and employs 975 in three locations, 280 at the Kirkland plant.

Plant Facilities Manager—March 1988 to present

Responsible for all aspects of plant and production engineering including facilities and machine maintenance, quality control, cost reduction, safety, and environmental concerns. Develop and maintain budget of approximately $8 million annually. Participate in daily management and long-range planning of plant operations. Introduced quality program that was later expanded to all company locations. Supervise 35 employees: 10 engineers, Maintenance Supervisor, and Purchasing Agent; 7 technicians and 16 hourly employees. From February-April 1991 was acting Plant Manager during illness of incumbent.

Chief Project Engineer—November 1984 to March 1988

Responsible for supervision of all projects including planning, budgeting, and decision making, with an engineering budget in excess of $5 million. Inaugurated team approach to all engineering functions; later extended to all production units. Supervised project engineering staff of four engineers and three technicians. Implemented plant improvements for cost savings, efficiency, and automation.

Project Engineer—July 1981 to November 1984

Responsible for project design, initiation, and supervision of both in-plant and outside labor. Projects included building modification and installation of equipment such as material handling systems for powder, dust control units, and automatic weigh systems. Emphasis was on automation and cost control.

Frank L. Stone Page 2

EDUCATION:

B.S. in Mechanical Engineering with Honors, Missouri Tech University, 1981; McMinn Scholarship, 1980-1981

Licensed Professional Engineer, State of Missouri, 1983

Advanced study in statistical analysis, personnel management and business administration, University of Missouri at St. Louis, 1984–1987

PERSONAL:

Married, two children

Excellent health

Canadian citizen, U.S. resident status since 1974

REFERENCES:

Excellent references furnished on request

Figure 14.2 Resume of Frank Stone.

If you send a cover letter and resume to several companies, the letter could be uniform in content. However, it is worth a few minutes' extra time to individualize at least a few sentences of each letter. Your company research should make that easy. One or two brief comments that indicate you have done your homework before contacting the company about employment are all that you need. As examples, look at the cover letters Janet Logan and Frank Stone will be sending.

Sample Cover Letter for Janet Logan

The cover letter Janet Logan sends inquiring about employment possibilities, not only to the firm that currently has an opening but also to others she contacts, makes clear the reason for her interest in the company. In a brief sentence or two of her letter to Woodford/Metier International, she indicates the attraction of the company's management training program and her qualifications as a candidate for a position as well as a prospective member of a management trainee group. Her comments make clear her awareness of the company's foreign activities and her interest in a period of employment abroad (see Figure 14.3).

The time Janet Logan has spent researching this company, making sure that it offers what she wants in her future career and that her qualifications meet its needs, should enhance her chances of obtaining an employment interview. If she is offered a position after her interview, her research and the additional information she gathers during the interview should make it easy for her to make a decision about accepting employment.

Sample Cover Letter for Frank Stone

Frank Stone has several years of professional experience, is familiar with other companies in his industry, and hopes to move to a senior management position in one of them. His letter notes his accomplishments with his present employer, particularly those that he has discovered will strike a responsive chord with a prospective employer. He also comments briefly on his reasons for seeking a new position (see Figure 14.4).

2333 Maple Street
Oakdale, Illinois 67777
May 8, 1992

Mr. Marcel Carrier
Chief Financial Officer
Woodford/Metier International
101 State Street
Chicago, Illinois 60611

Dear Mr. Carrier,

I read with great interest your advertisement for an entry-level position in the financial division of your firm in my college placement office. As my qualifications closely match your stated needs, I would like to be considered for the position.

I am a recent graduate of Oakdale University where I majored in accounting with special emphasis on financial accounting and accounting information systems. Because of a personal interest in international business affairs, I also took a directed research course in international accounting and business law. My interest in international business was furthered by a summer study course in Spain that focused on European commercial practice and by my study of French, Spanish, and Portuguese languages. I am fluent in spoken and written French, both colloquial and formal, and hope soon to be equally comfortable in Spanish. One of my personal goals is to develop expertise in European financial practice and, eventually, to work abroad.

I am particularly interested in the management training opportunities your company offers. My career goal is a management position and I believe my leadership skills in establishing a student chapter of the Association of Accountants and a volunteer student tax advisory service on my campus, as well as my volunteer community activities, are good indications of my potential for a position of responsibility.

I would be pleased to have an opportunity to discuss this position with you. Thank you for your consideration and I look forward to hearing from you.

Sincerely yours,

Janet E. Logan

Figure 14.3 Cover letter of Janet Logan.

3220 Walnut Street
Kirkland, Missouri 62111
June 14, 1992

Willard Brown, President
Deco-Tile Corporation
19001 Deco-Tile Lane
Cleveland, Ohio 41111

Dear Mr. Brown,

I have recently decided to seek a senior level management position and I understand from a mutual friend, George Herbert, that you will shortly be seeking a manager for a new plant in the Toledo area. I am very interested in this position and would appreciate your consideration as a candidate.

I hold a B.S. degree in Mechanical Engineering from Missouri Tech and have graduate credits in business administration from the University of Missouri, St. Louis, plus 12 years' experience in the manufacture of ceramic brick. Presently I am Plant Facilities Manager at Patriot Brick where I participate in managing the daily operations of a plant employing 280 workers and supervise an engineering division staff of 33. Over the years, I have had particular success in introducing a company-wide quality control program and a divisional work team approach to both engineering and production staff. As you may know, cost control has also been a hallmark at Patriot.

Growth opportunities at Patriot Brick are limited, and I have decided to pursue career options in other sectors of the ceramic processing industry. I have long admired the innovative record of Deco-Tile and would value an opportunity to be associated with one of the leading companies in the field. I believe I am well qualified to move into a position as Plant Manager and would like to meet with you to explore how I might contribute to your organization.

I can be reached on a confidential basis during the day at (314) 555-0055 or during the evenings in my home at (314) 555-6781.

Thank you for your consideration and I look forward to hearing from you.

Sincerely yours,

Frank Stone

Figure 14.4 Cover letter of Frank Stone.

THE EMPLOYMENT INTERVIEW

Browse through the shelves of a library or bookstore or visit the college placement center—you will find many excellent guides to employment interviews. Usually these guides review standard interview questions and suggest appropriate dress. Many of these books even discuss good postinterview behavior—the correct form of follow-up calls and thank-you letters. Rather than repeat that advice here, let's consider your strategies for effectively using company research in an interview.

During an interview, you can put your knowledge of a prospective employer to work. You will be prepared for the interviewer's questions and can enhance your qualifications by emphasizing those factors in your background and experience that your research has shown will interest the company. As the interviewer proceeds through standard questions—Why are you interested in this company? What skills would you bring to the position? What are your long-range career goals?—you can frame your answers to show that you have studied the company, have a genuine interest in it, and, indeed, can be an asset if hired. Remember, the interview is a chance to sell yourself, and the more you know about the buyer—the company—the better you will be able to market your product—you.

The interview is a time for both you and the interviewer to assess how you might fit into the company. Let the interviewer take the lead in telling you about the company. Use this opportunity to learn more about the company, not to impress the interviewer with your knowledge of the firm. Be sure, also, to listen carefully to what he or she says, for the information you have gathered may be dated or incomplete. You may want to modify your responses to the interviewer's questions, based on the new facts you are learning about the company.

Toward the end of the interview, you will usually be able to ask questions. Spend some time before the interview going over the information you have collected and jot down three or four topics you might ask about. By doing your homework before the interview, your questions can directly address issues that the company currently faces. You can also get information to fill in gaps in your previous knowledge of the company or clarify doubts you may have about accepting employment, if it is offered. It's acceptable to show that you have done some research, but, again, don't flaunt your knowledge.

Ask pointed rather than general questions of the interviewer. This will show that you have a genuine interest in the company, and you are also more likely to get direct answers. However, don't put the company's interviewer on the spot by asking, for example, what excuse the company will give shareholders to explain a recent 20 percent drop in earnings, or what defense it will use when called before the Environmental Protection Agency to testify on recent chemical spills. Ask, instead, for an assessment of the company's long-term financial outlook in light of recent recessionary trends. Ask about its corporate policy regarding government regulations on environmental hazards. Ask about specific products and the company's market strategies. Request more information on the company's highly successful quality assurance program. In other words, ask for the information necessary to evaluate the company, but be tactful in framing your questions. With advance preparation and courtesy, you should be able to get the information you want without making a bad impression.

Don't hesitate to ask where you will fit into the company's overall plans. If management training programs exist, ask if you are eligible. If you have learned that many employees leave the company after two or three years, ask about opportunities to get involved in meaningful projects shortly after being hired. If the company is small and entrepreneurial, ask about chances to grow with the company. If you are considering a small corporate division that, based on your research, looks rather weak, ask what your future with the corporation might be if the division were phased out.

Most interviewers will respond freely to direct questions, but don't probe if they seem reticent on certain points. If you advance through the interview process, you will have a second chance to ask any lingering questions and the company will often be more cooperative about providing information. And, finally, don't sell a product you can't produce. If your background does not match up exactly with the company's needs, be honest about what you have accomplished in the past and what you can offer in the future. Neither you nor the company will want to discover that your employment decision was a mistake after you have been hired.

ACCEPTING A POSITION

If you are offered a position with a company you have carefully researched, that same research can help you decide whether to accept the position. You will have new information gathered at your interview, you will have met your prospective supervisor and co-workers, and you will have seen your workplace. Step back now and analyze your own immediate and long-term goals.

Based on all you have learned, does this company have the potential to help you realize your goals? Will you have an opportunity to develop new skills and enhance existing ones? Based on expert opinion as well as the company's own assessment, what is the outlook for the future? Are problems the company has encountered in the past likely to recur or has it restructured or otherwise changed its pattern of response? Are the obstacles and challenges you expect as an employee unique to this company or typical of its industry? Did any information you gathered during the interview disagree with what your research told you to expect?

You may not be able to resolve all your questions but you should not have significant doubts. If your overall assessment of the company is positive, accept the position offered. Your company research has paid off and you can enjoy your new job!

Index

Illustrations are denoted by boldfaced page numbers.